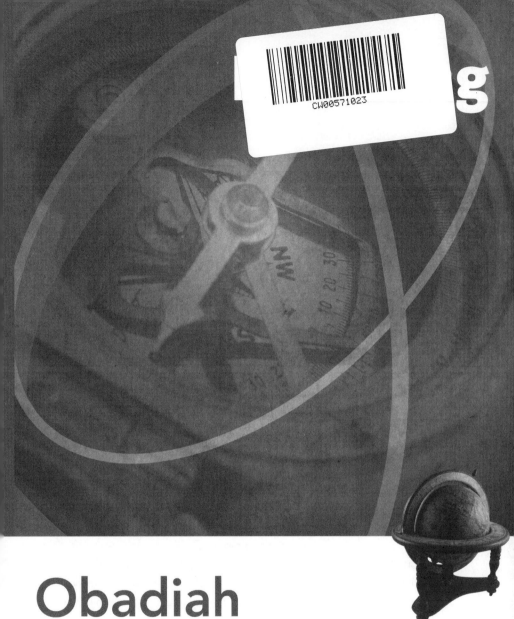

Obadiah
A practical commentary

David Field

DayOne

© Day One Publications 2008
First printed 2008

ISBN 978–1–84625–146–7

Unless otherwise indicated, Scripture quotations are from **The Holy Bible, English Standard Version (ESV)**, copyright © 2002 by Collins. Used by permission. All rights reserved.

British Library Cataloguing in Publication Data available

Published by Day One Publications
Ryelands Road, Leominster, HR6 8NZ
☎ 01568 613 740 FAX 01568 611 473
email—sales@dayone.co.uk
web site—www.dayone.co.uk
North America—email—usasales@dayone.co.uk

Cover design by Wayne McMaster
Printed by Gutenberg Press, Malta

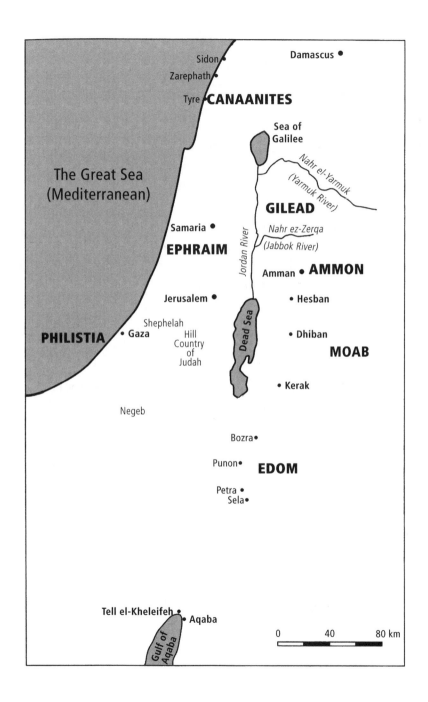

BC

c.930	division of the kingdom under Solomon
722	fall of the 10 northern tribes (Israel) and their exile into Assyria
587	fall of the 2 southern tribes (Judah), destruction of Jerusalem, captivity into Babylon
583	attacks from Nebuchadnezzar on Edom
553	attacks from Nabonidus on Edom
536–516	Jews return from exile in Babylon and rebuild the temple
c.450	Malachi declares that Edom has been judged
400–320	Nabataean migrations cause displacement of Edomites
135–104	reign of John Hyrcanus, during which the Edomites/ Idumaeans are forcibly circumcised

AD

30–70	the 'defeat of the (Edomite/Idumaean) Herods' by Jesus and the gospel
70/135	the destruction of Jerusalem and desolation of the land, after which nothing more is ever heard of Edomites/Idumaeans

Appreciations

David Field has managed, in a slim volume, to give us a number of things:
- *a commentary that takes the text of Obadiah seriously and explains it carefully*
- *a resource for all Bible teachers who are preparing to unpack this neglected book*
- *a study guide for individuals and groups who want to mine for gold here*
- *a brief master class in how to do biblical theology.*

Amazingly, he does it in clear prose which is peppered with helpful quotations from other authors. And he writes with a passion for Jesus Christ and God's coming kingdom that draws the reader to worship.

John Tindall, Associate Pastor of Monyhull Church, Kings Norton, Birmingham, England

Obadiah, like many short books, is densely packed with the truths of God. In this book, in equal measure scholarly and pastoral, David Field does wonderful work in unpacking those truths and showing their relevance for Christians today.

Doug Wilson, Pastor of Christ Church, Moscow, Idaho, USA, and author of Blog and Mablog

Contents

A CHRONOLOGICAL TABLE OF EVENTS **4**

INTRODUCTION **7**

1. AN OVERVIEW OF OBADIAH **15**

2. PRIDE GOES BEFORE A FALL (VV. 1–4) **25**

3. NOTHING CAN HELP YOU NOW (VV. 5–9) **38**

4. A DEVASTATING CHARGE SHEET (VV. 10–14) **52**

5. JESUS IN OBADIAH (1): THE MASTER STORY (VV. 10–14) **64**

6. JESUS IN OBADIAH (2): FAITH, HOPE AND LOVE (VV. 10–14) **73**

7. INTERNATIONAL JUSTICE(VV. 15–16) **82**

8. PUTTING THE WORLD TO RIGHTS (VV. 17–21) **90**

9. JESUS IN OBADIAH (3): OBADIAH AND THE GOSPEL (VV. 17–21) **102**

10. JESUS IN OBADIAH (4): OBADIAH'S DREAM (VV. 17–21) **110**

OBADIAH IN SONG **119**

APPENDIX 1 WHO IS BEING ADDRESSED IN OBADIAH 16A? **120**

APPENDIX 2 ACTS 2, JOEL 2 AND OBADIAH 17 **124**

FURTHER RESOURCES **127**

Remember, O Lord, against the Edomites, the day of Jerusalem,
how they said, 'Lay it bare, lay it bare, down to its foundations!' (Ps. 137:7)

In 587 BC, the Jews saw the city of Jerusalem fall to the Babylonians and the temple, built by Solomon nearly 400 years before, destroyed. The experience of this devastating judgement was made all the more bitter because the Edomites, their brothers and next-door neighbours, not only did not come to their aid, but, far worse, they also rejoiced in their humiliation, mocked their pain, looted their goods and handed over their survivors to the Babylonians. The book of Obadiah is a prophecy, probably given shortly after the fall of Jerusalem, which tells of the judgement upon Edom and the restoration of God's people.

It is said that 'the best things come in small packages,' and certainly the book of Obadiah bears that out. Weighing in at just twenty-one verses, it is packed full of good things: rich theology, powerful imagery, unsettling challenges to our thinking and living, and huge promises for the triumph of God's purposes. Obadiah uses key biblical themes, such as mountains and brothers, the kingdom of God and the day of the LORD; he challenges his hearers and readers by what he says about malice, pride and complacency; he encourages God's people with the promise of their sure inheritance; and he raises wider matters of justice, spiritual warfare and the international spread of the kingdom of God. Furthermore, like all the prophets, Obadiah again and again points us to the kindness and justice of the Lord Jesus Christ and to the greatness of what he has done for us.

Brother-to-brother relations

It will help us to understand the book of Obadiah and how we may learn from it if we think of the world as being like the face of an archery target.

The bullseye is the 'garden sanctuary', the centre of the world, where the people of God relate directly to God. The next ring out is the 'land', where the people of God relate to those who are close to them in what might be called brother-to-brother relationships. And the outer ring is the 'world', where the people of God relate to other human beings who are more distant from them (those outside the covenant) and to the wider environment.

So there are three zones: garden sanctuary, land and world. And there are three key relationships: with the Father, with the 'brother' and with the outsider.[1]

The people of God are called to faithfulness in all three zones and relationships. The book of Genesis can be seen as organized around these zones. The first fall (Gen. 3) takes place in the garden sanctuary, the second in the land as a brother-to-brother sin (Gen. 4) and the third in the world with the outsiders (Gen. 6). The cycle is then replayed as the Abraham story focuses upon the setting up of sanctuaries and the importance of trusting the Father; the Jacob story focuses upon the brother-to-brother rivalry and the importance of wrestling with and growing up as the Son; the Joseph story focuses upon connection with the wider world and the importance of faithfulness in the Spirit.

This way of looking at things gives us a key question to apply to a given passage of the Bible or event in the Bible: is what we are looking at primarily a sanctuary matter (how God's people relate to him), a land matter (how God's people relate to their 'brothers') or a world matter (how God's people relate to outsiders)?

When in 587 BC Jerusalem, the capital city of Judah, was destroyed by the Babylonians, it was as punishment for the sins of God's people and with the Edomites rejoicing and making things worse. After the event, there were various ways of describing what had happened, depending upon which zone or relationship was being considered:

- In 587 BC, Judah's sins of idolatry were punished by God.
- In 587 BC, God's people were mocked and hurt by their 'brothers'.
- In 587 BC, the Babylonian outsiders defeated God's unfaithful people.

The book of Obadiah does not mention the sins of Judah or the destruction of the temple—it is emphatically not a 'sanctuary' book about the relationship with the Father. Similarly, no mention is made of the Babylonians or of what to do in exile—Obadiah is not a 'world' book about the relationship with the outsider.

Rather, the book of Obadiah is all about the Edomites—about their pride, self-reliance and malice. This is a 'land' book about relationship with the 'brother'. But who is this 'brother' (see vv. 10,12)? The whole book is spoken to or about Edom. But who is Edom?

Jacob and Esau/Israel and Edom

Edom was the nation which grew from Esau. The story of the twin brothers Esau and Jacob, the younger of whom, Jacob, was destined by God to rule the elder, is well known, along with the incidents of Esau selling his birthright to Jacob and Jacob deceiving his father Isaac into giving him, rather than Esau, the blessing due to the firstborn. Relations between the two nations which grew from Jacob (later known as Israel) and Esau (father of the Edomites) were rarely any better.

Bible dictionaries and encyclopaedia give more detail, but David Baker summarizes the main data carefully and succinctly:

The land of Edom, also called Seir (Gen. 32:3; 36:20–21,30; Num. 24:18), lay south and east of the Dead Sea from the Wadi Zered to the Gulf of Aqabah. Straddling the Arabah rift valley running south from the Sea of Galilee to the Gulf of Aqabah, on the east it was rocky and mountainous, at times reaching c. 1,070 metres in elevation. Through it passed two major traffic routes, the King's Highway and the road along the Arabah. Its control over much of the north-south trade fed its coffers and made it a target for attack.

The Bible portrays the Edomites as descendants of Esau (Gen. 36, esp. vv. 1,9) ... After the Exodus, Israel was denied passage through Edom (Num. 20; Judg. 11:17–18) and shortly thereafter Balaam predicted Edom's conquest (Num. 24:18). Battle was joined with Edom under Saul (1 Sam. 14:47) and the area was conquered under David (2 Sam. 8:13–14 with RSV, NIV margin; 1 Kings 11:15–16) and exploited under Solomon (1 Kings 9:26–28), though not without Edomite opposition (1 Kings 11:14–22). In the ninth century, Edomites, in confederation with Moabites and Ammonites, raided Judah during Jehoshaphat's reign (2 Chr. 20:1–2). Edom more successfully rebelled against Jehoram (Joram) and enjoyed relative freedom from Israelite domination for about forty years (2 Kings 8:20–22; 2 Chr. 21:8–10).

Early in the next century, Judah under Amaziah retook Edom with great slaughter (2 Kings 14:7; 2 Chr. 25:11–12), advancing as far as Sela. Some time later, when Judah was itself under pressure during Ahaz's reign, Edom raided Judah, taking captives (2 Chr. 28:17), and shook herself loose from Israel, never to be subjugated to her again.

During the Assyrian period, from at least 734 BC, Edom was a vassal of Assyria and subsequently also of Babylon. At times they at least planned rebellion (Jer. 27) though there is no evidence of trying to realize these plans. The situation at the time of the fall of Jerusalem (587 BC) is not clear from either biblical or extra-biblical sources. 1 Esdras 4:45 blames the Edomites for burning the Jerusalem Temple, but this is unconfirmed (cf. Lam. 4:21–22).

In the sixth century, Edomite power waned, as indicated by archaeological remains, with an apparent abandonment of some towns and migration of population (cf. 1 Macc. 5:65). From the late sixth to the fourth centuries BC, Arab influence in the region was predominant (for indications of their presence in this period, cf. Neh. 2:19; 4:7; 6:1). This was brought to bear especially by the Nabataeans. Edomites were displaced. Some Edomites settled in the Negev in southern Judah, which became known by the related name Idumaea (1 Macc. 4:29).

Much of this reconstruction is based on conjecture and secondary sources, since documentation and archaeological evidence from the area itself is sparse and ambiguous.[2]

See the 'Study questions' section below for some of the leading references to Esau and Edom in the Bible.

Some key themes

Obviously, it is only through the actual study of the book of Obadiah that we can reach conclusions about what might be its principal themes. Nevertheless, by way of orientation and summary, some can be listed here:

1. The book of Obadiah is about the Lord Jesus Christ:
- He is God's own, humiliated and then vindicated.
- He is the Seed of Abraham, the true Israel.
- He bore the suffering described in verses 10–14 and embodies the righteous possession and rule described in verses 17–21.
- He perfectly lived out the opposite of all the Edomite sins, bore the penalty for those sins as committed by his people, and increasingly eliminates those sins from his people.
- He is the Lord who is outraged by mistreatment of his people and who will punish the persecutors of the church.
- He is the one whose coming constitutes the ultimate 'day of the LORD' and who will judge all the nations.

2. The book of Obadiah is about our spiritual fathers—how they suffered and how God would intervene to relieve and vindicate them.

3. The book of Obadiah is about the spread of the gospel to all the nations in the power of the Spirit.

4. The book of Obadiah is about the justice of God—how he knows and hates all sin and wickedness, judges with perfect justice and punishes with perfect appropriateness.

5. The book of Obadiah is about the particular wickedness of those who have been privileged by their closeness to the people of God and who should have known better than to persecute those people. The post-Christian media in the West; the Protestant-persecuting Roman Catholic and Orthodox Churches in some countries; Muslims who persecute Christians: all of these

have enjoyed the privilege of being related to the church of Jesus Christ and thus their malice towards the church is all the more reprehensible.

6. The book of Obadiah is more generally about how, when we are in close relationship to a person, we have an extra obligation to sympathize with and support that person when he or she suffers.

7. The book of Obadiah teaches us the particular wickedness of arrogant, self-reliant pride, which constitutes a challenge to God.

8. The book of Obadiah illustrates some of the key ways in which the second great commandment (to love our neighbours as ourselves) can be broken (the sin of neutrality, the studied avoidance of obligation, indifference to suffering, envy, malice, boasting).

9. The book of Obadiah shows us where family feuds, grudges and the profane spirit (living for self and for the here and now) lead.

10. The book of Obadiah teaches us that all things other than refuge in the true God will let you down.

11. The book of Obadiah shows that God is sovereign over the nations—to use them, judge them and punish them.

12. The book of Obadiah shows us that God intervenes in history to punish wicked nations, especially those that set themselves against the Lord and his people.

13. The book of Obadiah gives us a picture of what the world set straight looks like—definitively, in the work of the Lord Jesus; progressively, through history; and finally, in the new heavens and the new earth.

14. The book of Obadiah shows us that God uses individuals and nations as instruments of his purposes, even though those individuals and nations are themselves flawed.

15. The book of Obadiah shows us that hurting God's people is a very, very dangerous thing to do.

16. The book of Obadiah shows us that God keeps his promises to protect his people and to bless the world through his people.

17. The book of Obadiah shows us that the persecuted people of God

are to be confident in his care for them, even though they may feel neglected and hopeless.

A summary of Obadiah

v. 1—God's message to Edom through Obadiah (which is already being enacted) is:

vv. 2–4—'I will bring you proud Edomites down.

vv. 5–9—'Your devastation will be total, and your allies, wisdom and military might will not be able to prevent it.

vv. 10–14—'I will do so because of your malicious and treacherous behaviour towards Judah and …

vv. 15–16—'… this judgement will happen as and when I step in to judge all the nations.

vv. 17–21—'But my people will be delivered and, as agents of judgement, will defeat you Edomites—and they will take possession of their inheritance, exercising righteous rule over Edom.'

A word about this book

After a chapter which gives a full interpretative paraphrase of the book of Obadiah—attempting to make clear the flow and argument of the prophecy—and some study questions, which are necessary to work through if the reader is fully to benefit from what follows, there are nine further chapters. Five of these (Chapters 2, 3, 4, 7 and 8) run through sections of Obadiah explaining the words on the page and the main argument of each section. When a word which Obadiah uses will be more fully understood by referring to other places in the Old Testament where the same word is used, I have usually provided a list of such references. In these chapters (along the way in the comments but especially through the study and discussion questions), I try to show how the section of Obadiah under consideration should make an impact on the thinking and living of Christians today. Convinced that we have not properly understood and applied an Old Testament prophetic book unless it has taken us to the Lord Jesus Christ (see Luke 24:27; Acts 3:24), I have included four chapters (5, 6, 9 and 10) which give fuller attention to some of the ways in which we see the Lord Jesus Christ in the book of Obadiah.

There is a great deal more to be said about Obadiah than can be said in this short study guide. I have therefore listed some further resources at the end of this book.

Study question

Obadiah is a prophecy against the Edomites, who were the descendants of Esau, the brother of Jacob/Israel. Read the following passages. What can be learned from them about the Edomites and about their relationship with God's people? Genesis 25:19–27; 27:1–45; 32:1–33:16; 36:6–9,20–21; Numbers 20:14–21; 24:18; 33:37,41–44; Deuteronomy 2:4–8,12; 23:7–8; 33:2; Judges 5:4; 11:17; 1 Samuel 14:47; 2 Samuel 8:12–14; 1 Kings 3:9; 9:26–28; 11:14–22; 2 Kings 8:20–22; 14:7; 2 Chronicles 20:1–2; 21:8–10; 25:11–16; 28:16–19; Psalm 79; 83; 137; Isaiah 34; 63:1–6; Jeremiah 27; 49:7–22; Lamentations 4:21–22; Ezekiel 25:12–14; 35:1–15; Amos 1:11–12; 9:11–12; Malachi 1:2–5; Romans 9:10–13; Hebrews 12:15–17.

Notes

1 See **James B. Jordan,** *Through New Eyes* (Brentwood, TN: Wolgemuth & Hyatt, 1988) and **Peter J. Leithart,** *A House for My Name* (Moscow, ID: Canon Press, 2000) for further exploration of this idea.

2 **David W. Baker** in **David W. Baker, T. Desmond Alexander, Bruce K. Waltke,** *Obadiah, Jonah and Micah* (TOTC; Leicester: IVP, 1998), pp. 21–22.

An overview of Obadiah

Before plunging into the details of the various sub-sections of Obadiah, this chapter simply gives a further overview of the whole book. As you read it, jot down some of the ways in which you think that the book of Obadiah points us to the Lord Jesus Christ and some of the ways in which it addresses the sins and the needs of individuals, churches and nations today.

(v. 1) *The vision of Obadiah.*
This is the way that Obadiah sees things because this is what the LORD has revealed to him.

Thus says the Lord GOD concerning Edom ...
Obadiah's vision (the revelation he's received and the way that he sees things) not only flows from and agrees with, but also actually consists of and announces what God has to say to or about Edom.

We have heard a report from the LORD,
and a messenger has been sent among the nations:
'Rise up! Let us rise against her for battle!'
Reassurance is given to the defeated and oppressed Jews that what must seem impossible (the humbling and punishment of proud Edom) will most certainly happen. The process has already started; the events are already beginning to happen. God is stirring up the nations to go to war against Edom.

(v. 2) *Behold, I will make you small among the nations;*
you shall be utterly despised.
Now the LORD actually addresses Edom and tells this proud nation what it does not want to hear and will not believe, namely, that he will cause it to be humiliated before and despised by the nations.

(v. 3) *The pride of your heart has deceived you,*
you who live in the clefts of the rock,
in your lofty dwelling,
who say in your heart,
'Who will bring me down to the ground?'

Edom is convinced that it is safe, but it is wrong. Proudly confident that their rocky terrain and impenetrable secure places make them invulnerable to attack, the Edomites are sure that whatever threats are made, no one will be able to defeat or humiliate them.

(v. 4) *Though you soar aloft like the eagle,*
though your nest is set among the stars,
from there I will bring you down,
declares the LORD.

Edom's sense of security is a false one. What Edom says to itself is heard by God, loud and clear, and God accepts it as a challenge. God will not let that sort of attitude and talk pass without a response. He will bring down those who set themselves up in pride.

(v. 5) *If thieves came to you,*
if plunderers came by night—
how you have been destroyed!—
would they not steal only enough for themselves?
If grape gatherers came to you,
would they not leave gleanings?
(v. 6) *How Esau has been pillaged,*
his treasures sought out!

The devastation which is coming upon the Edomites is total. Whereas night-time burglars would take only the most valuable items, and even the most diligent gleaners would not find or pick all the grapes on the vine, when God sends judgement upon Edom there will be nothing left of its treasures or the things in which it takes pride or finds security. So complete is this judgement that it elicits two mock laments from God: 'how you have been destroyed! ... How Esau has been pillaged!'

(v. 7) *All your allies have driven you to your border;*
those at peace with you have deceived you;
they have prevailed against you;
those who eat your bread have set a trap beneath you—
you have no understanding.

The Edomites have a number of political and military alliances. They have entered covenant, sharing bread in a confirmation meal, with various surrounding tribes or nations and felt themselves to be at peace with them. But they have been deceived. Under pressure from Babylon perhaps, and stirred by the work of God (in whose hands are the hearts of kings), these nations, far from helping Edom when it comes under attack, will act treacherously, refusing to give help and, in a way, joining in the attack. The Edomites will be bewildered and dismayed by this, not understanding what is going on.

(v. 8) *Will I not on that day, declares the* LORD,
destroy the wise men out of Edom,
and understanding out of Mount Esau?
(v. 9) *And your mighty men shall be dismayed, O Teman,*
so that every man from Mount Esau
will be cut off by slaughter.

So much for the famed Edomite wisdom! It doesn't work, and even to the extent that there are wise men in Edom and there is understanding in Mount Esau, God will bring it to nothing. A day is coming—the 'that day' of God's judgement.

Similarly, the military strength in which the Edomites have placed their hope will prove useless. With the political and military leaders, normally so astute, having lost their grip on things, the strong will be panicked into feebleness. The result will be slaughter. The Edomites will be destroyed.

(v. 10) *Because of the violence done to your brother Jacob,*
shame shall cover you,
and you shall be cut off for ever.

What was it that provoked such judgement to fall upon Edom from God? The answer, in a phrase, is that the Edomites had acted violently towards the Jews, their brothers. The ways in which they did this are explained in the following verses, but here a summary of the punishment is announced: the Edomites will be humiliated (so much for their pride) and destroyed. Never again will Edom vaunt itself like this.

(v. 11) *On the day that you stood aloof,*
on the day that strangers carried off his wealth
and foreigners entered his gates
and cast lots for Jerusalem,
you were like one of them.

Another 'day' is referred to—not the day when God will judge the Edomites (v. 8) but the day when the Edomites committed the sins for which they are to be punished. It was a day of distress for Jacob, Judah and Jerusalem, a day when property was stolen, the city invaded and desecrated and the people shared out as slaves as if by lot. Of all days, that was the day when the Edomites should have sided with their brothers, the Jews. Their loyalties should have been shown that day. And they were—but, wickedly and tragically, those loyalties lay with the enemies of God's people rather than with God's people themselves. The Edomites had the attitudes, spoke the words and took the actions of those who were afflicting and maltreating the Jews. In fact, the Edomites 'were like one of them'.

(v. 12) *But do not gloat over the day of your brother*

in the day of his misfortune;
do not rejoice over the people of Judah
in the day of their ruin;
do not boast in the day of distress.
(v. 13) *Do not enter the gate of my people*
in the day of their calamity;
do not gloat over his disaster
in the day of his calamity;
do not loot his wealth
in the day of his calamity.
(v. 14) *Do not stand at the crossroads*
to cut off his fugitives;
do not hand over his survivors
in the day of distress.

Obadiah, speaking the LORD's words, revisits that day—the day of the Jews' misfortune, distress, calamity and disaster. He sees what the Edomites did and he cries out, forbidding them from doing these things. Even though the events themselves now lie in the past, the way Obadiah speaks gives them an immediacy and intensity.

There is a progression in this list. First, there is the Edomites' looking with indifference or pleasure at the suffering of God's people (gloating, rejoicing). This leads to mocking and boasting. Next the Edomites enter the city (v. 13) and there take another look of malicious pleasure at the Jews' suffering (gloat), after which they go around stealing the belongings of the Jews (looting). Finally, having done their worst in the city, the Edomites go back outside and stand at the very places passed by the Jews as they try to escape the Babylonians, in order to round up these refugees and hand them over to the Babylonians (v. 14).

(v. 15) *For the day of the LORD is near upon all the nations.*

As you have done, it shall be done to you;
your deeds shall return on your own head.

When will this punishment fall upon the Edomites? And how can God's people be sure that it will?

God's answer is that he is going to intervene personally in history on something called 'the day of the LORD'. He declares that this is imminent, inescapable and universal, and that it is therefore impossible for the Edomites to avoid it. All their wickednesses will return to them and they will certainly get their 'reward'.

(v. 16) *For as you have drunk on my holy mountain,*
so all the nations shall drink continually;
they shall drink and swallow,
and shall be as though they had never been.

How will this happen? Well, just as at the time of the fall of Jerusalem, the Edomites drank in mad and wicked revelry on Mount Zion, so when God steps in, all the nations will drink. God will force the nations to keep drinking and keep drinking and keep drinking. Maddened and drowned by this drinking, they will collapse, nevermore to rise. And Edom, of course, shall be among them, suffering the punishment for its sins.

(v. 17) *But in Mount Zion there shall be those who escape,*
and it shall be holy,
and the house of Jacob shall possess their own possessions.

But on that day, in that intervention of God the Judge, there will also be escape, survival, deliverance. In the very place where God makes himself known as Judge to all the nations, Edom included, he will make himself known as Saviour to his people. The very place which saw Edom's grotesque wickedness will be set apart by God as his holy dwelling place. And this act of salvation and restoration will result in the people of God possessing their promised inheritance.

(v. 18) *The house of Jacob shall be a fire,*
and the house of Joseph a flame,
and the house of Esau stubble;
they shall burn them and consume them,
and there shall be no survivor for the house of Esau,
for the LORD has spoken.

Rescued and restored, God's people will also be empowered and will become instruments in his hand for the setting right of all wrongs, the punishment of wickedness and the utter defeat of evil. Evil Edom will be annihilated.

(v. 19) *Those of the Negeb shall possess Mount Esau,*
and those of the Shephelah shall possess the land of the Philistines;
they shall possess the land of Ephraim and the land of Samaria,
and Benjamin shall possess Gilead.
(v. 20) *The exiles of this host of the people of Israel*
shall possess the land of the Canaanites as far as Zarephath,
and the exiles of Jerusalem who are in Sepharad
shall possess the cities of the Negeb.

A further description of the time of restoration and renewal follows, framed in terms of God's people taking possession of lands all around, leading to the establishment of an extensive empire. To the south (19*a*), to the west (19*b*), to the north (19*c*) and to the east (19*d*), lands which have been lost or compromised will be recovered. Verse 20 states the same again: one set of exiles will take over the land to the north (20*a–b*), and another set will take over the land to the south (20*c–d*).

(v. 21) *Saviours shall go up to Mount Zion*
to rule Mount Esau,
and the kingdom shall be the LORD's.

And at the heart of this rescued and restored people and this recovered and expanded territory will be Mount Zion itself. Spirit-empowered leaders and rescuers will ascend it and from there exercise rule over that 'kingdom' which has acted so wickedly to the Jews in the past. In the battle of mountains, Zion wins and the kingdoms of this world have become the kingdom of the LORD. He is the one who occupies the throne and exercises righteous royal power. That is exactly how it should be and that is certainly how it shall be. Glory to God!

Study questions

Here are a number of brief questions which will require a closer look at the text of Obadiah. Although some of the questions which follow may initially seem rather simple, they are designed to help the reader carefully to attend to the *details* of the text of Obadiah so as to benefit more fully from the rest of the study. I suggest 'answers' in the chapter endnotes.

1. Who is the prophecy from?[1] Who is it about/to?[2] Which people are mentioned?[3] Which places are mentioned?[4] Which words seem to come up quite a few times?[5]

2. How many times do the following words occur: 'the LORD', 'day', 'Esau'?[6]

3. What, if any, is the progression of the sins in verses 12–14?[7]

4. Find some sort of word or thought link between the following pairs of verses:[8]

(a) 1b & 18f

(b) 1d & 2a

(c) 3e & 4c

(d) 4d & 8a

(e) 5a–d & 5e–f

(f) 5c & 6a

(g) 7b & 3a

(h) 7e & 8c

(i) 8c & 9b

(j) 9b & 10c

(k) 16b & 15a

(l) 17a & 14c

(m) 17b & 16a

(n) 17c & 19a–d, 20b, 20d

(o) 19a & 20d

(p) 21a & 17a

(q) 21b & 8c, 9b, 19a

(r) 21c & 1b

5. This is a book about contrasting *mountains*. What is its message concerning these mountains?[9]

6. This is a book about contrasting *days*. What is its message concerning these days?[10]

7. This is a book about contrasting *brothers*. What is its message concerning these brothers?[11]

8. What are the different things in which Edom could be said to place trust in (a) verse 6; (b) verse 7; (c) verse 8; (d) verse 9?[12]

9. What are the different perspectives on *who* it is that brings Edom down in (a) verses 1–2; (b) verses 4,8; (c) verse 7; (d) verse 18?[13]

10. What are the different perspectives on what happens to Edom in (a) verse 7; (b) verse 19; (c) verses 9,18; (d) verse 21?[14]

11. What are the images used in the book in (a) verse 4*a*; (b) verse 4*b*; (c) verse 5 (x 2); (d) verse 10*b*; (e) verse 11*d*; (f) verse 16*a–b*; (g) verse 18*a–d*?[15]

12. Put the following statements in order according to how accurately you think they present the main thrust of Obadiah. Compare your order with someone else's order and discuss your reasons.

- God is sovereign over the nations.
- Pride deceives people and is hateful to God.
- God will judge betrayal, malice, envy, boasting, indifference and *schadenfreude*.
- The goal of history is the kingdom of God.
- Family feuds are the cause of terrible grief.
- God's action and human actions are intertwined.
- God keeps his promises.
- Hurting God's people is very dangerous.
- God will secure justice—describing the crimes of the guilty, announcing the verdict and the sentence and promising vindication and compensation for the innocent.

Chapter 1

Notes

1 The Lord through Obadiah.

2 Edom.

3 See vv. 1,6,10,17–18.

4 See vv. 1,8–9,11–12,17,19–21.

5 Edom, Esau, the Lord, Jacob, day, 'do not', nations, distress, calamity, possess, Mount.

6 'The Lord': seven times (it is translated as 'God' in several translations of v. 1); 'day': twelve times; 'Esau': seven times. Putting those three together, we could say that Obadiah teaches that 'because of a day and on a day [12 times], the Lord [7 times] will defeat and judge Esau [7 times].'

7 Standing watching, gloating, rejoicing, entering the city, looting, preventing escape, handing over escapees.

8 (a) Says the Lord; (b) nations; (c) bring down; (d) declares the Lord; (e) if … if … ; (f) how … how … ; (g) deceived; (h) understanding; (i) Mount Esau; (j) cut off; (k) all the nations; (l) survivors/escape; (m) holy; (n) possess; (o) Negeb; (p) Mount Zion; (q) Mount Esau; (r) the Lord.

9 Vv. 8–9,17,19,21a. In the battle of the mountains, Zion comes to rule over Esau.

10 Vv. 8,10–15. In the contrast of the days, the wickedness of the Edomites on the 'day' of Judah's calamity will be repaid on the 'day' of the Lord.

11 Vv. 10,12,17–18. In the contest of the brothers, the false and treacherous firstborn will have to submit to and serve the younger son.

12 (a) Hidden treasures; (b) allies; (c) wisdom; (d) military might.

13 (a) The Lord using the nations; (b) the Lord; (c) the allies; (d) Israel. When vv. 15–16 are added to this, we see that the Lord punishes Edom, that he uses the nations to do so, that he uses Israel to do so and that he punishes the very nations which he uses for their own sins.

14 Edom is (a) displaced; (b) dispossessed; (c) left with no survivors; (d) ruled over righteously. These ways are, of course, complementary rather than contradictory.

15 (a) Soaring like an eagle; (b) nesting among the stars; (c) being burgled and being gleaned; (d) being clothed in shame; (e) having lots cast for possessions; (f) drinking judgement; (g) God's people being a flame and the wicked being burned up like stubble.

Pride goes before a fall (vv. 1–4)

The child on the tree-stump chants, 'I'm the king of the castle.' The arrogant football coach claims that his team is unbeatable. The totalitarian dictator announces a thousand-year empire. And we know, for a certainty, what will happen to all three. 'Pride goes before … a fall' the proverb tells us (Prov. 16:18), and major Bible stories have shown us exactly that: Adam and Eve's desire to be like God plunged them and the world under the curse (Gen. 3); Nebuchadnezzar boasted insufferably and was turned into an animal (Dan. 4:28–33). The opposite is also true: because Jesus humbled himself, God highly exalted him and gave him a name above every name (Phil. 2:5–11). ✐

In the book of Obadiah, after the title and the book's purpose is stated, along with a reassurance about its certain fulfilment (all in v. 1), we see the same pattern played out in the Edomites. With haughty over-confidence the Edomites ask, 'Who will bring me down?' and with settled resolve and unstoppable intent God replies, 'I will bring you down.'

A title and an assurance (v. 1)

Verse 1 has five lines. The first two lines give the title and the origin of the book, and the next three lines (which should be read as though they are in brackets) give an assurance that the fulfilment of the prophecy against Edom is certain because God has already set it in motion.

(v. 1a) *The vision of Obadiah*

A 'vision' is a revelation from the LORD and is one way of describing the message which God gives to a prophet (see also Isa. 1:1 and Nahum 1:1).[1]

'Obadiah' is the name of a dozen or more different people in the Old Testament. It means 'a servant or worshipper of the LORD'. If, as is likely, the prophecy is given in response to the Edomites' behaviour at the fall of Jerusalem in 587 BC, then we know nothing more about this Obadiah than we find in this book. The Puritan commentator John Trapp says, 'Let him be who he will (for where the Scripture hath no tongue, we need not find ears, but may content ourselves with a learned ignorance).'[2]

(v. 1b) Thus says the Lord GOD concerning Edom
These first two lines are a little like the beginning of Paul's letters. They provide 'authentication' and amount to a statement that the following message really does come from God and must be heard as such.

THUS SAYS THE LORD GOD ...
This is the way that prophetic 'oracles' are often introduced. It emphasizes that this is God's message, not merely the prophet's.

Two words are used for God—one means 'Master, Lord' and the other is the name of God (*Yahweh*, which in most English translations is indicated with the capitalized word 'LORD'). Put together, this underlines that the LORD, Israel's God, is the Master, so he has authority and power to pronounce and effect the judgement on Edom which is coming.

The name of God, the LORD (*Yahweh*), occurs seven times in the book of Obadiah:
- 'Thus says the Lord GOD' (v. 1)
- 'a report from the LORD' (v. 1)
- 'declares the LORD' (v. 4)
- 'declares the LORD' (v. 8)
- 'the day of the LORD' (v. 15)
- 'the LORD has spoken' (v. 18)
- 'the kingdom shall be the LORD's' (v. 21)

It can be seen from this that the LORD's name is used in order to underline the source and authority of the words of the prophecy and to highlight the key message of the prophecy—that the LORD who is king will intervene in judgement and deliverance, with the result that his kingship will be acknowledged and experienced.

... CONCERNING EDOM

This could be translated as 'to Edom' or 'about Edom'. In fact, both are true. The words on the page are spoken as if to the Edomites ('I will make *you* small' etc.), but the intended hearers are the exiled Israelites. This is called 'apostrophe'—speaking words as if to hearer A when the intention is that hearer B should get the message. For example, with her son in the room and using a loud voice, the young boy's mother says to her friend, 'He's *such* a good boy, you know,' with the full intention that, although she is talking to her friend, actually the encouraging message will really be received by her son. So God addresses Edom, but the message is really for his people.

(v. 1*c*) *We have heard a report from the* LORD,
(v. 1*d*) *and a messenger has been sent among the nations:*
(v. 1*e*) *'Rise up! Let us rise against her for battle!'*

The people of God were devastated by the vicious Edomites. But God has given a word to Obadiah to deliver to Edom, and the people of God are hearing it for their own encouragement. But what hope is there really for its fulfilment? The Israelites are a broken people, and the Edomites seem secure in their rocky strongholds, enjoying plundered goods and laughing still at Israel's disaster. What assurance can be given to the people of God that the prophecy of judgement about to be delivered will really be fulfilled?

These three lines of verse 1 give that assurance: in brief, that God has already begun the process of judgement. The button has been pressed. The wheels have been set in motion. God is already stirring up the nations to take military action against Edom.

There are three difficult questions of interpretation relating to these lines which should be mentioned, although there is not space fully to discuss them:

Who are the 'we' of 1c?

There are several possibilities:

- Obadiah is using a royal 'we', speaking for himself alone.
- Obadiah is speaking for Jeremiah and himself, since a large part of Obadiah is a restatement and application of a prophetic word which Jeremiah had given some years before (see Jer. 49:7–22).
- Obadiah is speaking as a member of God's council of prophets—those who stand before God, participate in God's deliberations and are then commissioned to speak those words effectively and authoritatively in the world in order to make things on earth conform to God's decisions in heaven (see Jer. 23:18–22; 1 Kings 22:13–23; Gen. 18:17; 20:7; Amos 3:7–8).
- Obadiah is speaking as though there is more than one messenger because, when important news was to be conveyed in the ancient world, more than one messenger would be sent so that, first, there would be more chance of the message getting through and, second, once it did get through, the message's authenticity could be checked by comparing the versions from two or more different messengers.
- Obadiah is speaking for God's people who have, perhaps, gathered for worship and have, during that worship, heard a message from another prophet or from the Scriptures.

What is the relationship between 1c and 1d?

The possibilities are:

- We have heard the news *that* a messenger has been sent to the nations.
- We have heard the news *because* a messenger has been sent among the nations and it came to our ears too.
- We have heard the news *and* a messenger has been sent among the nations.

Who is the messenger of 1d?

This person could be:

- a political or military envoy sent from a great power, such as Babylon, to the surrounding vassal nations to command them to take up arms against Edom. This messenger would be doing what he was doing because God had made it happen, but he may not have been aware of the fact.
- an angel or spirit sent from God to incite the nations by moving the hearts of kings and counsellors to decide upon action against Edom.
- a prophet sent by God to command various nations to act against Edom.

Although these questions are difficult ones, still the thrust of the second half of verse 1 is clear: the people of God should be in no doubt that God will take action against the Edomites because things have already started happening. The news is out. The messengers have already been sent. The nations surrounding Edom are stirring and preparing themselves to military action against her.

WE HAVE HEARD A REPORT ...

The word 'report' simply means 'something heard', be it news, tidings, a report or a rumour. (The word is used elsewhere in the Bible in places such as 1 Sam. 2:24; 2 Kings 19:7; Ps. 112:7; Isa. 53:1; Jer. 10:22; 51:46.)

... AND A MESSENGER[3] HAS BEEN SENT AMONG THE NATIONS

'The nations' are mentioned four times in Obadiah:

- 'a messenger has been sent among the nations' (v. 1)
- 'I will make you small among the nations' (v. 2)
- 'the day of the LORD is near upon all the nations' (v. 15)
- 'all the nations shall drink continually' (v. 16).

It is clear in the book of Obadiah that the LORD is sovereign over all the earth. He can send messengers around the nations (v. 1), take actions that are seen by the nations (v. 2), draw near in judgement upon all the nations

(v. 15) and punish all the nations (v. 16). The nations can be instruments or spectators or the objects of God's judgement. The Edomites thought that the Israelites were all alone among the nations but that they themselves had allies (v. 7). But they reckoned without God, who could turn the nations against them.

'RISE UP! LET US RISE AGAINST HER FOR BATTLE!'

This is the content of the message which has gone around the nations. They are to rise up for battle against Edom. The words 'rise' and 'arise' are used for a call to military action (see Deut. 2:24; Josh. 8:1; Judg. 4:14; 5:12; 18:9; Micah 4:13. The call for battle itself is similar to that in Isa. 21:5; Jer. 6:4–5; 49:14,28,31; Joel 3:9–13). It is as if God is saying, 'I am going to take action against the Edomites and I am going to use you nations as my instruments. Up we get, it's time to be about our business.' God marches out at the head of the armies. He is the commander-in-chief.

... AGAINST HER

It is worth pointing out that, although some English translations smooth things out, the pronouns used for Edom and the Edomites vary a little through the book. This can be illustrated just from the first two verses. Sometimes Edom is addressed as 'you' (v. 2), and sometimes it is referred to as 'him' or 'her' (v. 1). Sometimes Edom can be feminine (v. 1) and sometimes masculine (the Hebrew forms behind the 'you's and 'your's of vv. 2–3 are all masculine). Sometimes Edom is singular (vv. 1–2) and sometimes plural (v. 16, if the first 'you' is Edom).

Proud Edom is not beyond the reach of God's judgement (vv. 2–4)

After the introduction of 1a–b and the reassurance of 1c–e, the LORD actually addresses the Edomites, telling them that they will be humiliated before and despised by the nations. This is just what a proud Edom does not want to hear and will not believe.

(v. 2a) Behold, I will make you [I have made you] small among the nations;

(v. 2b) you shall be [are] utterly despised.

I WILL MAKE YOU [I HAVE MADE YOU]

Many of the statements in Obadiah are, in the original Hebrew, in the perfect tense, which is often used to report what has happened in the past. This is not because the judgement of the Edomites has already happened but because Obadiah is using a standard way of speaking called the 'prophetic perfect'. It is a way of expressing the fact that that which has been predicted is so sure and certain that it is virtually accomplished already. It is rather like one boxer muttering to the other 'You're dead' or 'You've lost' as they enter the ring before the fight has even begun.

I WILL MAKE YOU SMALL

The particular form of Edom's judgement is its devastation as a nation. It will lose territory, population, security, favour with other nations and its reputation. Edom will become a nonentity, not in the sense of ceasing to exist in every respect but of being utterly insignificant—not even on the radar screen, as we might say.

... DESPISED

This word is used around forty times in the Old Testament and has to do with being rejected and being regarded with contempt. (Some of its occurrences include Gen. 25:34; Num. 15:31; 1 Sam. 2:30; 10:27; 2 Sam. 6:16; 12:9; 2 Kings 19:21; 2 Chr. 36:16; Neh. 2:19; Esth. 1:17; Ps. 22:6; 51:17; 69:33; 102:17; 119:141; Isa. 53:3; Jer. 22:28.) One of these usages is particularly striking—that of Isaiah 53:3. Edom and the suffering servant (the Lord Jesus Christ) experience the same thing—smitten by God, they are despised by others.

(v. 3a) The pride of your heart has deceived you,

(v. 3*b*) *you who live in the clefts of the rock,*
(v. 3*c*) *in your lofty dwelling,*
(v. 3*d*) *who say in your heart,*
(v. 3*e*) '*Who will bring me down to the ground?*'

THE PRIDE OF YOUR HEART HAS DECEIVED YOU

The Edomites are so pleased with themselves. They are convinced that they are militarily secure because so much of their territory is made up of craggy, impenetrable fortresses and fastnesses. Douglas Stuart comments, 'In addition to Sela, Edom's main cities of Teman and Bozrah, as well as the nascent fortress city of Petra nearby Sela, were located in nearly impenetrable high rock formations reached only by narrow, vulnerable gorges in each instance.'⁴ (They are also pleased, perhaps, about their wealth (v. 6), their alliances (v. 7), their wisdom (v. 8) and their mighty men (v. 9)—more on this below.)

But they are badly mistaken. Theirs is a false sense of security, and God is going to show them the truth of their vulnerability and weakness before long. They *are* proud, but they *will be* despised (v. 2).

How did they come to believe the lie of their own invincibility? It was through pride. In their hearts (the intellectual and emotional centre of a person or, in this case, a nation) they thought of themselves more highly than they ought, and this has misled them into complacency. They have presumed that they are greater and, especially, more secure than they really are. But, as Calvin says, 'It is the greatest madness for men to rely on their own power and to despise God himself.'⁵

PRIDE

The Hebrew word used here could be translated as 'presumption', 'insolence', 'arrogance' or 'pride'. (Some of the other places where it is used in the Old Testament include Deut. 17:12; 18:22; 1 Sam. 17:28; Prov. 11:2; 13:10; 21:24; Jer. 50:31–32.)

... OF YOUR HEART

What is in the heart is known to God. Our thoughts and feelings are like things that we 'say' inside us, but God has excellent hearing; what we say in our hearts, he hears loud and clear.

... DECEIVED YOU

The same word is used in verse 7. The Edomites are deceived first by the pride of their own hearts and then later by their allies. Such deception often leads to disaster—as it certainly did in Genesis 3! Eve claimed in Genesis 3:13 that 'The serpent *deceived* me ...', and John Trapp comments on the use of the word in Obadiah verse 3 that what is being said to Edom is 'thy pride hath befooled thee and put the same trick upon thee that the serpent did once upon the first woman'.[6] (See also 2 Kings 18:29; Isa. 19:13; Jer. 29:8; 37:9.)

... LIVE [DWELLER/DWELLING] IN THE CLEFTS OF THE ROCK [CRAG]

The word for 'rock' here is the same as the name of a major Edomite town, Sela (Judg. 1:36; 2 Kings 14:7), as well as a high and strong rock or cliff (1 Sam. 13:6; 2 Sam. 22:2; Job 39:28; Ps. 40:2; 104:18; Prov. 30:26; Isa. 2:21; 7:19; 33:16), and it is therefore probably intended as a deliberate play on words.

... IN YOUR LOFTY DWELLING [THE HEIGHT OF HIS DWELLING]

This phrase may simply mean 'the height in which he is situated', or possibly it is intended to convey thoughts of a lofty throne, a seat in the heavenlies, an exalted residence. If the latter, it would reinforce the idea that the Edomites regarded themselves as occupying a place superior to that of others, as well as living at higher altitudes. (The word translated in the ESV as 'lofty' is the noun 'height', which is used around fifty times in the Old Testament. Some of its other occurrences include 2 Sam. 22:17; 2 Kings 19:22–23; Job 5:11; Ps. 7:7; 68:18; 73:8; 92:8; 102:19; 148:1; Isa. 26:5; 33:5; 57:15; Jer. 51:53.)

Chapter 2

'WHO WILL BRING ME DOWN TO THE GROUND [EARTH]?'

Words of this sort amount to a challenge to God. Coggins comments that it is 'characteristic of the condemnation of foreign nations to draw attention to their false boasting'.7 This is the sort of vaunting of oneself which marked out Goliath in the Valley of Elah (1 Sam. 17:8–10,26,44), the Assyrians in the eighth and seventh centuries BC (Isa. 2:6–22; 10:5–19) and Nebuchadnezzar on his palace roof in Daniel 4. In each instance, pride went before a fall.

'Who *will* bring me down?' amounts to 'Who *can* bring me down?' The question is intended to be rhetorical and thus unanswerable. But where the Edomites expected an awed silence, they actually get the thunder voice of God taking up the challenge in verse 4.

(v. 4*a*) *Though you soar aloft like the eagle,*

(v. 4*b*) *though your nest is set among the stars,*

(v. 4*c*) *from there I will bring you down,*

(v. 4*d*) *declares the* LORD.

IF YOU MAKE YOURSELF AS HIGH8 AS THE EAGLE,
IF YOUR NEST IS SET IN THE STARS ...

It makes no difference how high the Edomites are: high in their rocky fortresses; higher still—up with the soaring eagles; higher still—nesting in the stars. In fact, the higher they go, the more vulnerable they are. Not only do they have further to fall, but also, metaphorically, the higher up they are, the more likely they are to be noticed by God! Climbing high, far from putting a person or power beyond the reach of God, brings that person or power to his notice. This is what happened, for example, with those building the tower and city of Babel in Genesis 11.

EAGLE

(It is possible that this refers to the vulture.) The eagle was known for flying high, for nesting high, for looking down and for being a ruthless predator (Exod. 19:4; 2 Sam. 1:23; Ps. 103:5; Isa. 40:31; Lam. 4:19; Hosea 8:1). But God himself knows how to eagle (Deut. 32:11), and so there will be no getting away from him.

STARS

Up in the heavens, the stars are the choir and the court of God. Do the Edomites really think that they can have a place among the stars or that, if they can, they will be beyond God's reach? God made the stars, and he can not only reach the stars, he can also use them as his armies and instruments and cause them to fight against his enemies.

Setting oneself up high in the stars is like the action and attitude of the Babylonian king in Isaiah 14. As Wolff puts it, 'Edom emulate[s] the plan of the Babylonian king who, according to Isa. 14:12–14, desires to place his throne above the stars.'[9] (See also Isa. 14:15 and Num. 24:21.) This is one of several links between Obadiah and Amos (see Amos 9:2–4a).

BRING YOU DOWN

This is a translation of the same word the Edomites used in their hearts in verse 3 when they asked, 'Who will bring us down?' Here, as in a number of other places in Obadiah, we see that the punishment fits the crime.

Matthew Henry sums up: 'If men will dare to challenge Omnipotence, their challenge shall be taken up.'[10]

DECLARES THE LORD

This phrase (also in v.8) serves both to show that verses 2–4 are a distinct unit and to confirm that what has been said represents not the idle hopes of a disempowered prophet but the firm resolve of the sovereign God.

Study questions

1. How do the examples used in this chapter (Adam and Eve in Gen. 3;

the tower of Babel in Gen. 11; Goliath in 1 Sam. 17; Assyria in Isa. 2 and 10; Nebuchadnezzar in Dan. 4) reinforce the teaching of Obadiah verses 2–4?

2. Consider any relevant parallels between the teaching about the fall of Satan in Luke 10:18 and Revelation 12:7–11 and the teaching of Obadiah verses 2–4. (What is said about the king of Babylon in Isa. 14:12–21 and the king of Tyre in Ezek. 28:1–19 is similar.)

3. Take time to ponder the ultimate example of the opposite of Obadiah verses 2–4, namely, that if someone humbles him- or herself, then God will exalt that person (see Phil. 2). Now apply that to the importance of Christian humility (see Matt. 20:26–28; 23:11–12; Luke 14:7–11; John 13:1–17; James 4:10; 1 Peter 5:5–6).

4. What do you know about the character and the word of God that makes anything introduced by the words 'thus says the LORD' *so* powerful and relevant?

5. What would need to be true about God's character and purposes in history and about human sin and needs for prophecies given about Edom around 2,600 years ago to be relevant to us? Are those things true, and how do you know?

6. Does God still exercise his rule over the nations, using them to fulfil his purposes of grace and wrath? Give some possible instances.

7. Identify some of the most secure 'powers' (persons or institutions or nations) of our day—financial, political, academic, military or opinion-forming powers. Think of some of the ways in which those powers speak proudly. Apply (in discussion and in prayer) Obadiah verses 2–4 to those powers.

8. Can local churches be 'proud', setting themselves up, being pleased with themselves and regarding themselves as more secure than they really are? If so, how can this be avoided? (Consider Rev. 3:14–22.)

9. How might Obadiah verses 2–4 be an encouragement to the persecuted church? Pray for oppressed Christian brothers and sisters in the light of this.

10. Why is pride such a challenge to God? Is God being touchy or oversensitive?

11. What impact does it have upon you to consider that God hears everything you 'say in your heart'? (See also Mark 2:8; Heb. 4:12; Rev. 2:23.)

Notes

1 'Vision' is not necessarily to be thought of as distinct from receiving the 'word' of the LORD. On the one hand, a 'word' can be seen because it is also an event: see Num. 24:3–4,15–16 and Hab. 2:1. On the other hand, a vision can be heard: see Ps. 89:19. Some other places in the Old Testament where this word is used are 1 Sam. 3:1; Prov. 29:18; Jer. 23:16; Lam. 2:9; Ezek. 7:26; 12:27; Hosea 12:10; Micah 3:6.

2 **John Trapp,** A Commentary or Exposition upon the XII Minor Prophets (London, 1654), p. 292.

3 Other places where this 'messenger' word is used include 1 Sam. 4:19; Prov. 13:17; 25:13; Isa. 18:2; 57:9.

4 **Douglas Stuart,** Hosea–Jonah (Word Biblical Commentary; Waco, TX: Word Books, 1987), p. 417.

5 **John Calvin,** Commentaries upon the Twelve Minor Prophets, vol. ii: Joel, Amos, Obadiah, trans. John Owen (Edinburgh: Calvin Translation Society, 1846), Lecture LXIX, p. 427.

6 **Trapp,** Commentary, p. 293.

7 **Richard J. Coggins,** Israel Among the Nations: A Commentary on the Books of Nahum and Obadiah (International Theological Commentary; Grand Rapids, MI: Eerdmans, 1985), p. 79.

8 Other places in the Old Testament where this word is used and which give a flavour of the Edomite claim are 2 Chr. 26:16; 32:25; 33:14; Job 36:7; 39:27; Ps. 103:11; 131:1; Prov. 18:12; Isa. 7:11; 52:13; 55:9; Ezek. 17:24; 21:26; 28:2; 31:10; Zeph. 3:11.

9 **Hans Walter Wolff,** Obadiah and Jonah: A Commentary (Minneapolis: Augsburg Publishing House, 1986), p. 49.

10 **Matthew Henry,** A Commentary upon the Whole Bible, vol. iv (1712; [n.d.], Iowa Falls, IA: World Bible Publishers), p. 1271.

Nothing can help you now (vv. 5–9)

The ammunition has run out, the escape routes are closed and the defences have just been breached. The car is careering down the mountain road at 80 mph, the brakes have failed and the steering wheel has come off in your hands. The headmaster was standing there as you threw the first punch; he is now striding towards you at pace, and you are in a corner of the room with no doors or windows anywhere near you. Nothing can help you now.

So with the Edomites. Their false confidence has been exposed and their proud challenge taken up in verses 2–4. Now, in verses 5–9, two further dimensions of God's judgement are announced and described. First, in verses 5–6, the extent of the judgement is declared—it will be total. Second, in verses 7–9, all the possible escape routes are closed off—all those things to which Edom might have looked for help (allies in v. 7, wisdom in v. 8 and strength in v. 9) will prove useless. The coming judgement of Edom will be total and inescapable. Nothing can help the Edomites now.

Total judgement (vv. 5–6)

Verses 5–6 show the totality, the thoroughness, of God's judgement on the Edomites.

(v. 5*a*) *If thieves came to you,*
(v. 5*b*) *if plunderers came by night—*
(v. 5*c*) *how you have been destroyed!—*
(v. 5*d*) *would they not steal only enough for themselves?*
(v. 5*e*) *If grape gatherers came to you,*

(v. 5f) would they not leave gleanings?
In verse 5, two comparisons are given to show that, although destruction is not usually complete and total, this time it will be.

IF THIEVES CAME TO YOU, IF PLUNDERERS OF THE NIGHT

Thieves work secretly and plunderers work violently, but neither group takes everything that there is to take. The word translated 'plunderers' carries associations of a destroyer, deadly enemy or devastator, one who lays waste, who does violence or brings ruin or disaster (Job 15:21; Ps. 17:9; 137:8; Isa. 16:4; 21:2; Jer. 4:20; 48:8).

HOW YOU HAVE BEEN DESTROYED![1]

This exclamation interrupts what is being said about thieves and plunderers. It is a mock lament, rather like that in Isaiah 14:12 ('How you are fallen from heaven!'), and is meant to drive home how shockingly absolute the punishment of the Edomites will be. (Other examples of this way of putting things can be seen in Isa. 6:5; 15:1; Hosea 4:6. The use of 'How ...' like this can be seen in 2 Sam. 1:19; Isa. 14:4,12; Jer. 9:19.)

WOULD NOT THEY STEAL ONLY ENOUGH FOR THEMSELVES [THEIR SUFFICIENCY]?

Thieves and plunderers would eventually reach a point where they said, 'Enough!' Not so with God's judgement—there will be no limit to it.

IF GRAPE GATHERERS CAME TO YOU, WOULD THEY NOT LEAVE GLEANINGS?

Gleaning was the practice of letting the poor take what was left over after the harvest had been completed (see Lev. 19:9–10; Deut. 24:19–22). Even the most diligent harvester would leave something which the poor would be able to find. But not God in his coming judgement upon Edom. It would be total. Nothing would be left.

(v. 6a) How Esau has been pillaged,

(v. 6*b*) *his treasures sought out!*

God now speaks *of* Edom rather than *to* Edom. One commentator remarks that it is almost as though Edom is no longer there.[2]

HOW ESAU HAS BEEN PILLAGED,[3] HIS TREASURES SOUGHT [SEARCHED] OUT

A second exclamation beginning 'How …' reinforces the mock lament of verse 5.

'Esau', of course, stands for Edom, since Esau was the father of the Edomites (see Gen. 36:1,8,19).

With the words 'sought [searched] out' comes the idea of digging, mining or delving deep, in order that whatever there is to be discovered really will be discovered. The Edomites have hidden their treasures in rocky hideaways, but this will do them no good.

Calvin sums up the impression that these verses create:

We hence learn, that as men in vain seek hiding places for themselves that they may be safe from dangers; so in vain they conceal their riches; for the hand of God can penetrate beyond the sea, land, heaven, and the lowest deep. Nothing then remains for us but ever to offer ourselves and all our things to God. If he protects us under his wings, we shall be safe in the midst of innumerable dangers; but if we think that subterfuges will be of any avail to us, we deceive ourselves.

Allies, wisdom, strength are no help to the Edomites now (vv. 7–9)

As the total devastation of God's judgement over the Edomites is announced (vv. 5–6), the natural reaction of a people as proud as they are is to look to their own resources. It is as though, after verse 6, the Edomites reply, 'Yes, but we have our alliances, our wisdom and our mighty men … we will be able to avert, withstand, survive or recover from God's judgement.' Verses 7–9 come as an answer to that unspoken boast of the Edomites. As part of the description of the comprehensiveness of Edom's defeat, the three things upon which they most rely, far from averting judgement, themselves fall under that judgement.

Those three things are allies (v. 7), wisdom (v. 8) and military strength (v. 9).

(v. 7a) *All your allies have driven you to your border;*
(v. 7b) *those at peace with you have deceived you;*
(v. 7c) *they have prevailed against you;*
(v. 7d) *those who eat your bread have set a trap beneath you—*

Three groups are mentioned: literally, these are 'men of your covenant' (v. 7a), 'men of your peace' (v. 7b) and 'your bread' (v. 7d). All three of these refer to the same people, namely, the neighbouring tribes or nations with whom the Edomites have contracted peace treaties. They have a *covenant* with these peoples to guarantee *peace* which has been sealed by eating *bread* together in a covenant-confirming meal.

TO THE BORDER THEY HAVE DRIVEN [SENT] YOU, ALL YOUR ALLIES [THE MEN OF YOUR COVENANT]

This is the second 'sending' in the book and results from the first, which was mentioned in verse 1. Because God has sent a messenger around the nations, the nations will turn against Edom and will 'drive [send]' it away.

Exactly what is meant by 'to the border they have sent you' is difficult to establish. It probably means one of three things:

- The Edomites flee a hostile power and run for asylum to their allies. The allies refuse them asylum and send them back to the border of their own territory.
- Edom's allies are themselves the hostile force, and these allies drive the Edomites out of their own land, displacing them and pushing them to their own borders.

- Edom has sent messengers to its allies asking for help, but those messengers are themselves dismissed and escorted back to the edge of the allied territory.

Whichever of these is correct, the basic point is the same: far from being supportive allies, these tribes and nations have become enemies who fight against and act treacherously towards the Edomites, subduing them and trapping them.

The Edomites' alliances have done them no good. The very people who were to guarantee the peace and safety of the Edomites have deceived them, prevailed over them and set a trap under them. And there is an appropriateness about this. Just as Edom deceived itself by pride (v. 3), so now Edom is deceived by its allies. Just as Edom was treacherous at the time of the fall of Jerusalem (see vv. 10 and 14), so now Edom suffers treachery from its allies. And just as Edom's treachery took the form of not providing help when it was needed and of taking positive steps to harm the one who should be helped (see v. 11), so Edom now experiences this at the hands of its allies.

YOUR BREAD HAS SET A SNARE UNDER YOU

This literal translation appears not to make sense. It may well be that the text should read, 'those who eat your bread' (as the ESV puts it). Or it may be an extreme shorthand for 'those whose alliance with you has been sealed by a contractual meal'. It reminds us that in the Bible, alliances and contracts were sealed by eating together, and that these covenantal or sacramental meals were also found in human relationships with God at times such as the peace offerings, the meal halfway up Sinai in Exodus 24, sinners eating with Jesus, the Lord's Supper, the offer of Revelation 3:20, the banquet of the kingdom of God and so on.

Betrayal by those in alliance or covenanted together is seen elsewhere in Scripture. This was David's experience in Psalm 55:12–15, for example, and, most pointedly, in Psalm 41:9, which in the New

Testament is taken up with reference to Jesus. We read, 'Even my close friend in whom I trusted, who ate my bread, has lifted his heel against me.' But whereas treacherous Edom deserved all it got, the betrayal of the faithful Lord Jesus Christ was the worst of sins (see Luke 22:22; John 6:70; 13:18; 17:12).

SET A SNARE [TRAP]

This may be metaphorical and refer to the deception already described. Or it may be literal and refer, for example, to mantraps set at the Edomite border of the allied countries in order to deter Edomites from trying to escape into them. It is the only use of this word in the Old Testament, and some translations give it as 'wound' because they confuse it with another word.

The lessons here are that false alliances and reliances will always let a person or nation down if they are engaged in contrary to God's will. This is the trouble that comes upon a person or nation that resists and rebels against the supreme emperor. Those who oppose God think that they can cleverly arrange some scheme by which they will be protected against his judgement. They are wrong.

Two older commentators sum up much of what we learn here. John Trapp comments, 'Many friends are like deep ponds, clear at the top and all muddy at the bottom.'4 And Calvin remarks,

All the compacts then which the ungodly and the despisers of God make with one another, have always something vicious intermixed; it is therefore no wonder that the Lord disappoints them of their hope, and curses their counsels. This is then the reason why the Prophet declares to the Idumaeans [Edomites], that those, whom they thought to be their best and most faithful friends, would be their ruin.5

(v. 7e) *you have no understanding*

This phrase, too, could be interpreted in various ways. It might be quite general: 'So you see, there is no sense in this proud nation Edom—the people do not have the sense to realize that this is going to happen, nor do they have the ability to deal with it when it does.' Or it might be more specific: 'Edom will not be able to comprehend this betrayal.' Or it could be more specific still: 'Edom will not understand about the trap.' Because the pronoun used is 'him' (as footnoted in the ESV, following the Hebrew, although it was 'you' earlier in the verse) and because the rest of the verse leads up to this rather than depends upon it (the verse would 'work' even if this phrase were not here), it is probably best to see it as a stand-alone summary of the situation: 'clever' Edom is clueless, 'wise' Edom is witless. As Wolff puts it, 'The wisdom which would know how to avert the life-threatening danger can no longer be found in Edom.'[6]

The word translated 'understanding' forms a link to verse 8. It is used around forty times in the Bible,[7] and Deuteronomy 32:28 is particularly interesting, saying of disobedient Israel, 'For they are a nation void of counsel, and there is no understanding in them.'

> (v. 8*a*) *Will I not on that day, declares the* LORD,
> (v. 8*b*) *destroy the wise men out of Edom,*
> (v. 8*c*) *and understanding out of Mount Esau?*

WILL I NOT ... ?

Yet another question. The Edomites have asked a question in verse 3. There were two questions in verse 5. Now another question, probably put like this in order to reinforce the certainty of what is going to happen.

ON THAT DAY

This is the first reference to 'day' in the book of Obadiah. (In total, there are twelve uses of the word—in vv. 8, 11 (x2), 12 (x4), 13 (x3), 14 and 15.) There are two 'days' in view in the book. The first is the day referred to over and over again in verses 11–14—the day when the people of God suffered so much and the Edomites sinned so badly. The second is the day of the LORD's coming against all nations, mentioned in verse 15. It is this day which is the guarantee of Edom's destruction. The day of Edom's destruction is an instance, manifestation or instalment of the day of the LORD, and it is this second day which is referred to here in verse 8—the day when God will intervene in just judgement to punish the Edomites for their sins and to dismantle and destroy the nation.

Notice, though, that these two days are inextricably connected. It is *because* of the day of Edom's sin that the day of Edom's punishment is inevitable.

DESTROY THE WISE MEN OUT OF EDOM

As the attacking nations descend upon the Edomites, at just the time when Edom is in need of sound advice, God will scatter and disable the source of wisdom, leaving Edom helpless and exposed.

The 'wise men' are probably those in the royal court who have offered military and political counsel to the rulers. Without them, there will be no hope of effective relations with other nations or of proper political or military decision making. Some, on the basis of Job 2:11, Jeremiah 49:7 and 1 Kings 4:30, think that Edom was famous for its 'wise men' and that this related to its location on major trade routes and thus its access to new and sophisticated ways of thinking. If so, then God's explicit declaration that he would destroy the wise men serves only to underline the vulnerability of sinners, even at their strongest points, to God when he comes in judgement. Riches will not help the rich; neither will wisdom help the wise, nor might the mighty.

'Destroy' might mean either that the wise men will be killed or dispersed, or that they will lose their wisdom and so be unable to provide the counsel needed at a time of national crisis (see also Isa. 19:11–15).

UNDERSTANDING OUT OF MOUNT ESAU

The three times when Mount Esau is mentioned in Obadiah are the only occurrences of this name in the Bible. It is quite common in the Bible to refer to kingdoms by a dominant mountain within them, but with the Edomites, this is usually done using Mount Seir, so that when 'Seir' is mentioned, it is understood to be a reference to the Edomites. This can be seen in Ezekiel 35:2–3,7,15, for example. (Other key references include Gen. 32:3; 33:14–16; 36:8–9,21,30; Deut. 1:2,44; 2:1,4–5,12,22,29; Josh. 24:4; Judg. 5:4; 1 Chr. 4:42; 2 Chr. 20:10,22–23; 25:11,14; Isa. 21:11.)

In some ways, the whole story of redemptive history can be told as a battle between kingdoms and, therefore, between mountains. Something of this comes out in Psalm 68:15–16; Isaiah 2:1–5; Daniel 2:35,44–45; and Galatians 4:21–31. Here in Obadiah, the battle of mountains is between Mount Esau and Mount Zion. It is clear from this verse that God is sovereign in judgement over the kingdom of Edom; this means that the book can end with the promise that Mount Esau will be ruled from Mount Zion.

The world will end with the dominance of the mountain of the LORD over all other mountains and with the kingdoms of this world becoming the kingdom of our God and of his Christ.

Looking back over the whole of verse 8, Calvin's comments are, once again, apt:

Yet the worst blindness is, when men become inebriated with the false conceit of wisdom. When therefore any one thinks himself endued with understanding, so that he can perceive whatever is needful, and that he cannot be circumvented, his wisdom is insanity and extreme madness: it would indeed be better for us to be idiots and fools than to be thus inebriated. Since then the wise of this world are insane, the Lord declares that they will have no wisdom when the time of trial comes. God indeed permits the ungodly for a long time to felicitate themselves on account of their own acumen and counsels, as he suffered the Idumaeans to go on prosperously. And there are also many at this day who felicitate themselves on their successes, and almost adore their own cunning…

There is hardly one in a hundred to be found, who does not seek to be crafty and deceitful, if he excels in understanding. This is a very wretched thing. What a great treasure is wisdom! Yet we see that the world perverts this excellent gift of God; the more reason there is for us to labour, that our wisdom should be founded in true simplicity. This is one thing. Then we must also beware of trusting in our own understanding, and of despising our enemies, and of thinking that we can ward off any evil that may impend over us; but let us ever seek from the Lord, that we may be favoured at all times with the spirit of wisdom, that it may guide us to the end of life: for he can at any moment take from us whatever he has given us, and thus expose us to shame and reproach.

(v. 9a) *And your mighty men shall be dismayed, O Teman,*
(v. 9b) *so that every man from Mount Esau will be cut off by slaughter.*
Again and again in the Bible, the pair of 'wisdom and might' go together (see, for example, Dan. 2:20–23 and, indeed, the rest of that chapter, which is a conflict between Babylon's wisdom and power and God's might and power; see also 1 Cor. 1:18–31).

We are unsurprised, therefore, that, in addition to the destruction of Edom's wisdom, God announces the disempowering of Edom's might. This may be a direct consequence of the loss of the wise men—the military forces are lacking in strategic guidance and lose heart—or it may be relatively independent. But by the end of this verse, all four wheels have fallen off Edom's chariot—riches (v. 6), allies (v. 7), wisdom (v. 8) and might (v. 9)—and it now crashes down with no hope of recovery.

AND YOUR MIGHTY MEN SHALL BE DISMAYED, O TEMAN
The 'mighty men' are the military heroes, the elite troops, the warriors in whom the nation placed its confidence. They will be 'dismayed' (broken, demoralized, frustrated or caused to panic; see also Exod. 23:27; Deut. 7:23; 1:21; 31:8; Josh. 1:9; 10:10; 1 Sam. 2:10; 17:11; Job 7:14; 32:13; 39:22; Isa. 9:4; 30:31; 31:4,9; Jer. 8:9; 17:18; 23:4; 48:1,20,39; 50:2; 51:56).

'Teman' is another way of referring to the whole of Edom since it was one of Edom's major towns, named after one of Esau's grandsons (Gen. 36:9–14; 1 Chr. 1:35–36).

SO THAT EVERY MAN WILL BE CUT OFF [FROM THE MOUNTAIN OF ESAU] BY SLAUGHTER

Quite a lot of translations put 'slaughter' at the beginning of the next verse but there is no compelling reason to do this, as can be seen by comparing this verse with Genesis 9:11.

It is important to note that the phrase 'every man' is not to be taken literally. As Finley puts it, 'It must also be noted, however, that in Hebrew thought to speak of "all" or "every" often means a majority or a very large number. For example, David struck down "every male in Edom" (1 Kings 11:15), yet the nation of Edom continued.'[8]

Renkema raises the same point, mentioning

the hyperbolic character of the Ancient Near Eastern rhetoric of warfare in which terms such as 'always', 'for ever', 'total' are commonplace features. As such, therefore, Ob 2 does not intend to announce the total destruction of Edom but rather to predict Edom's future insignificance and contemptibility. Indeed, the expression 'they shall become as if they had never existed' at the end of Ob 16 implies a similar interpretation … The end in question is the end of Edom as a state … [T]he concluding verse Ob 21 … clearly does not presume total annihilation. The focus, rather, is on upright rule over the remaining inhabitants of the politically insignificant mountains of Esau by a series of redeemers who dwell in Zion.[9]

Quite apart from the importance of understanding the Bible writers' ways of expressing themselves, this is important because verse 21 itself implies that there will be something recognizable as 'Mount Esau' (which is emphatically a group of people rather than a geological feature) to be ruled over even after the judgement has taken place.

Malachi 1:3–4 helps us understand this further:

'... Esau I have hated. I have laid waste his hill country and left his heritage to jackals of the desert.' If Edom says, 'We are shattered but we will rebuild the ruins,' the LORD of hosts says, 'They may build, but I will tear down, and they will be called "the wicked country", and "the people with whom the LORD is angry for ever."'

At one and the same time, Esau will be a desolation though there would be some Edomites remaining. But God's determination is that they shall never rise again as a nation. And they never did.

Thus it is wrong to state, as one commentator does, that 'No known historical event included a disaster of the size portrayed here.'[10] The point is that God intervened in judgement in such a way that Malachi was able to speak of the decisive judgement having taken place. Whether his mind was focused primarily upon a military action of Nebuchadnezzar's against the Edomites in 583 BC, of which we know little, or of another action under Nabonidus in 553 BC, of which we know only a little more, or even of the Nabataean migrations which displaced the Edomites in the fourth century BC, it is hard to say. But, in spite of the continued existence of some people who could be recognized as Idumaeans, the people never existed as an independent national entity again and, indeed, in the second century BC they experienced forced circumcisions under Jewish dominance led by John Hyrcanus.

By the second century AD, with the work of the Lord Jesus Christ completed (and the repeated 'defeat' of the Idumaean Herods at the hands of Christ and his apostles) and its geopolitical outworking in the shaking of the world of Palestine and the surrounding area through AD 70 judgement and its AD 135 sequel, it would not have been possible to find people who identified themselves as Edomites or Idumaeans. The judgement which God declared in Obadiah had taken place by Malachi's day and was indisputable within 100 years of the resurrection of Jesus.

Obadiah 9, read properly, does not mean that there will be no single Edomite left alive. It means, as one commentator puts it, that 'a people once characterized by its own arrogance is to be left a nonentity in the international arena'.[11] Perhaps the best way of highlighting the reality of the historical judgement is simply to ask the question, 'When did you last meet an Edomite?' or to look up the Edomite embassy in the telephone book.

God's judgement of the Edomites, announced in Obadiah 5–9, was total and inescapable.

Study questions

1. List all the ways in which the punishment of the Edomites in Obadiah reflects their sins. How does God declare that 'the punishment fits the crime' in Obadiah?

2. What are the key mountains in the Bible, and in what way can the message of the Bible be summarized by telling the story of these mountains?

3. Look more closely at the way in which wisdom and might relate in Obadiah 8 and 9 and in the whole of Daniel 2.

4. The announcement of judgement in Obadiah 5–9 is terrifying, but no more so than Jesus' declarations of judgement in the Gospels (see, for example, Matt. 13:41–42; 18:6,8,34; 25:30,41). Since we live in a time and place of very little reflection upon the awfulness and horror of judgement, take time to ponder it now.

5. 'You cannot hide yourself or anything else from God. But you can hide yourself and all you treasure in God.' Illustrate this contrast from Scripture and consider its implications for your own life.

6. The Edomites' idols were allies, wisdom and strength, and this can be seen because they placed their hope or reliance in them. What are the key 'idols of our time' in the sense of things in which people put their hope to save them from one sort of disaster or another?

7. Does God punish nations today in the way in which he declared the judgement of the Edomites in Obadiah? If so, what, from Obadiah, do you think would be the main cause of that judgement?

8. In what are we tempted to put our hope, falsely—personally? as a local church? as a nation?

9. How might the book of Obadiah strengthen the hearts and hands of the persecuted church today? Compare it with the solemn verses of 2 Thessalonians 1:4–10 and 2 Peter 2:4–10.

Notes

1 'Destroyed' means ruined, silenced, ended, laid waste. See also Jer. 47:5; Zeph. 1:11.

2 **David W. Baker** in **David W. Baker, T. Desmond Alexander, Bruce K. Waltke,** *Obadiah, Jonah and Micah* (TOTC; Leicester: IVP, 1998). Comment on v. 6.

3 'Pillaged.' Isaiah used this word to describe the plundering of the hidden valuables of a conquered people. This word (and/or related words) is used in 1 Kings 20:6; Isa. 45:3; Prov. 2:4; Job 30:18; Gen. 44:12; Zeph. 1:12–13.

4 **John Trapp,** *A Commentary or Exposition upon the XII Minor Prophets* (London, 1654), p. 296.

5 **John Calvin,** *Commentaries upon the Twelve Minor Prophets*, vol. ii: *Joel, Amos, Obadiah,* trans. John Owen (Edinburgh: Calvin Translation Society, 1846), Lecture LXX, pp. 433–434.

6 **Hans Walter Wolff,** *Obadiah and Jonah: A Commentary* (Minneapolis: Augsburg Publishing House, 1986). Comment on v. 7.

7 Nearly twenty of these are in Proverbs. See also Exod. 31:3; Deut. 32:28; 1 Kings 4:29; Job 12:12–13; Ps. 49:3; 147:5; Prov. 2:2–3,6; Isa. 40:28.

8 **Thomas J. Finley,** *Joel, Amos, Obadiah: An Exegetical Commentary* ([n.p.]: Biblical Studies Press, 2003), p. 319.

9 **Johan Renkema,** *Obadiah* (Historical Commentary on the Old Testament; Leuven: Peeters, 2003), pp. 42–43.

10 **David J. Clark** and **Norm Mundhenk,** *A Handbook on the Books of Obadiah and Micah* (UBS Helps for Translators; London: UBS, 1982). Comment on v. 9.

11 **Renkema,** *Obadiah*, p. 40.

A devastating charge sheet (vv. 10–14)

Sometimes, those who are being rebuked or punished speak as though they are the ones offended against rather than the ones who have offended. In a hurt tone of voice they might ask, 'What have I done to deserve this?' not because they are claiming to be innocent but because they wish to shift the emotional burden away from themselves. But it is a dangerous tactic because it invites the reply, 'What have you done? What have you done? How dare you ask that? I'll tell you what you have done.' And what follows is the catalogue of wrongdoing and offence that brought the rebuke or the punishment in the first place.

Something of that sort is happening here in Obadiah as we move from the announcement of judgement in verses 5–9 to this next section, verses 10–14. It is as if, in response to the completeness and inescapability of the destruction described in verses 5–9, the Edomites have asked, 'What have we done?' and then, in verses 10–14, God replies, 'I'll tell you what you have done.' Edom's sins show that Edom utterly deserves the judgement it is to receive.

This section is made up of three smaller units. Verse 10 is a once-over summary of Edom's sins with a reiteration of the coming judgement. Verse 11 is another once-over summary, this time focused on showing how the Edomites took the wrong side at the crucial moment. Then verses 12–14 give a vivid denunciation, sin by sin, of all that the Edomites thought, said and did at the fall of Jerusalem, watching the events unfold and showing how the Edomites went from bad to worse during the time that the fall took place.

We have already seen that God makes the punishment fit the crime, and this is brought home again through these verses. Edom will be violated and robbed (v. 6) because Edom itself has violated and robbed (vv. 10,13). Edom will be attacked by allies and scattered (v. 7) because Edom itself has attacked and scattered others (vv. 12–14).

The application of these verses to individuals, local churches and nations can be shown at a number of levels (see Chapters 5 and 6 for examples). In general, however, this much is clear: in the sixth century BC, God hated the sins of the Edomites which are described in these verses. In the twenty-first century AD, he hates these sins still. As Wolff puts it, 'Obadiah's accusations (vv. 11–14) turn into new warnings, sentence by sentence, warnings against departing from the path of Christian discipleship.'[1]

(v. 10a) *Because of the violence done to your brother Jacob,*
(v. 10b) *shame shall cover you,*
(v. 10c) *and you shall be cut off for ever.*

BECAUSE OF THE VIOLENCE DONE TO YOUR BROTHER JACOB

This introductory phrase powerfully brings home how shocking was the Edomites' behaviour. 'Violence' should not go together with 'brother'; rather, 'love' should. And this was 'Jacob'—the personal name is used here for the first time in the book as a way of underlining the heinousness of Esau's behaviour.

The Hebrew word translated 'violence' is *hamas* (connected with the word we know as the name of a Palestinian terror organization) and stands for violence and wrong, often arising out of hatred and sometimes out of extreme wickedness. (Some other places where it is found in the Old Testament include Gen. 6:11,13; 16:5; Judg. 9:24; 2 Sam. 22:3; Job 16:17; Ps. 11:5; 27:12; 140:11; Prov. 16:29; Isa. 53:9; 60:18; Jer. 13:22; Joel 3:19; Hab. 1:2.)

SHAME SHALL COVER YOU

The image is that of being clothed in shame. (The other places in the Bible where this word is used are Ps. 89:45; Ezek. 7:18; Micah 7:10.) Back in verse 2, God said that he would make the Edomites become despised, and this phrase vividly conveys the same idea.

YOU SHALL BE CUT OFF FOR EVER

The Edomites will cease to exist as a recognizable and distinct (let alone rich, wise, mighty and proud) nation.

> (v. 11a) *On the day that you stood aloof,*
> (v. 11b) *on the day that strangers carried off his wealth*
> (v. 11c) *and foreigners entered his gates*
> (v. 11d) *and cast lots for Jerusalem,*
> (v. 11e) *you were like one of them.*

The 'day' of the Babylonian destruction of Jerusalem was the 'day' of the Edomites' sin. The Babylonians were the 'strangers' and 'foreigners' who violated the city, captured its wealth and divided up the people and possessions by lots. And just when the people of God might have hoped that their Edomite brothers would support them, the Edomites instead sided in attitude and action with the strangers and foreigners, standing aside to watch and subsequently joining in, maliciously and selfishly. The Edomites sided with the enemies of God's people just when they should have shown themselves friends of God's people. And this appals the LORD. That Edom should side with strangers and foreigners, with thieves and looters and invaders, rather than with 'brother Jacob' is a summary of its wickedness.

ON THE DAY THAT YOU STOOD ALOOF

The Edomites' posture was that of 'looking on', and their attitude was a combination of indifference to and approval of the suffering inflicted on and experienced by God's people (rather like Saul watching at the death of Stephen in Acts 7:54–8:1). They took no action but, rather like the priest and the Levite in the parable of the Good Samaritan (Luke 10:31–32), they kept away when neighbourly action was demanded.

ON THE DAY THAT STRANGERS CAPTURED [CARRIED OFF][2] HIS WEALTH AND FOREIGNERS ENTERED HIS GATES
Niehaus remarks, 'The passage of enemies through the gate signifies a city's loss of self-rule.'[3]

AND CAST LOTS FOR JERUSALEM
They divided the spoils of conquest by casting lots (see also Nahum 3:10; Joel 3:3; and, of course, Ps. 22:18 and John 19:24).

YOU [ALSO] WERE LIKE ONE OF THEM
The phrase is heavily stressed, almost as though it beggars belief: '*You also* were as one of them ...'

(v. 12*a*) *But do not gloat over the day of your brother*
(v. 12*b*) *in the day of his misfortune;*
(v. 12*c*) *do not rejoice over the people of Judah*
(v. 12*d*) *in the day of their ruin;*
(v. 12*e*) *do not boast*
(v. 12*f*) *in the day of distress.*
(v. 13*a*) *Do not enter the gate of my people*
(v. 13*b*) *in the day of their calamity;*
(v. 13*c*) *do not gloat over his disaster*
(v. 13*d*) *in the day of his calamity;*
(v. 13*e*) *do not loot his wealth*
(v. 13*f*) *in the day of his calamity.*
(v. 14*a*) *Do not stand at the crossroads*

(v. 14*b*) *to cut off his fugitives;*

(v. 14*c*) *do not hand over his survivors*

(v. 14*d*) *in the day of distress.*

The structure of these three verses is plain. There are eight loud commands of 'Do not X.' Seven of these are followed by the phrase 'in the day of Y' (and 12*a* also has 'the day of' so that 'day' is here eight times too). The commands are given as though they refer to the future, even though the events themselves have already taken place. This is probably for a number of reasons:

- By putting the past wicked actions of the Edomites in the form of commands in the present or future, the idea of God as a father or teacher (the two main figures who would speak like this) is brought into our minds; this underlines that what has taken place has been an outrage 'within the family'. This makes Edom the evil son who defies his father.[4]

- Giving these as commands to obey rather than descriptions of what happened emphasizes that Edom's conduct was a shocking transgression of perfect law.

- Various authors comment upon the rhetorical impact of putting it this way. Allen, for example, states,

The prophet shouts as if in the grip of a nightmare. He feels afresh the emotions of resentment and loathing as in his mind's eye he sees again the leering, loutish folk of Edom. In his anguish he screams out 'No, no, no!' protesting with all his being against their revelling in the situation that spelled the end of Judah.[5]

Intense emotion and careful literary structure are not mutually exclusive, as anyone who has read Lamentations or Gerard Manley Hopkins's desolation sonnets knows well.

Rather than work through these verses phrase by phrase, it is better to list first the ways in which the 'day' is described and then the various sins of the Edomites.

IN THE DAY OF …

'The day' of Judah's humiliation and Edom's sin is described in various
ways:

- his misfortune
- their ruin
- distress
- their calamity
- his calamity
- his calamity
- distress

Little comment is needed upon these terms.[6] A passage like this does not
need lots of definitions and cross-references. This was the most awful,
heart-rending, sickening day in which a nation, a city and thousands of
lives were torn apart. And on this day, to their undying shame, the
Edomites neither stood nor wept with the people of God.

Quite the contrary. The eight 'do not's describe what it was that the
Edomites did on that day:

- do not gloat [or look]
- do not rejoice
- do not boast
- do not enter
- do not gloat [or look]
- do not loot
- do not stand … to cut off
- do not hand over

There is a clear progression in these verses, both in terms of moving from
an internal attitude to external conduct and in some sort of chronological
sequence. Finley puts it like this:

This progression of watching, gloating, entering, looting, blocking escape, and handing
over refugees to the enemy is reinforced by the structure of the passage itself. In vv. 10

and 11 Obadiah reports the scene objectively, while in vv. 12–14 he directly admonishes the Edomites. These verses, in turn, have a structure that highlights the sequence that moves from outside (v. 12) to inside (v. 13) and then back outside the city (v. 14).[7]

Trapp makes a similar comment: 'Sin proceeds by degrees: neither is any man at his worst at first. First they looked at the church's calamity, and then they laughed, and then they insulted and spoke big words, and then they plundered, and lastly they butchered some and imprisoned other[s].'[8]

The particular sins warrant some brief comments.

DO NOT GLOAT [LOOK]

This is both the first term to be used and the only one which occurs twice. It is translated in various ways including 'gloat over', 'look down upon', 'gazed on', and 'looked on'. But although the term is very simple, it is a certain *sort* of looking which is condemned here and, from the way in which verse 12 develops, it is clear what sort of looking it was. The Edomites looked on at the 'day' of their brother and at his 'disaster' with something between indifference and pleasure: indifference, in the sense of caring not at all about Judah's suffering; pleasure, in the sense that there was malice, hatred, spite, vengefulness and the desire to benefit from the disaster (see also Ps. 22:17; 118:7; Micah 7:8). Matthew Henry comments, 'We must take heed with what eye we look upon the afflictions of our brethren; and, if we cannot look upon them with a gracious eye of sympathy and tenderness, it is better not to look upon them at all.'[9]

DO NOT REJOICE

The Edomites committed the sin that we call *schadenfreude*—a malicious pleasure in the misfortune of another. (See Isa. 14:8; Ps. 30:1; 35:19,24; Prov. 17:5; 24:17 for other examples of this.)

Two other important passages refer to the same moment. The picture in Psalm 137:7 is striking:

Remember, O LORD, against the Edomites
    the day of Jerusalem,
how they said, 'Lay it bare, lay it bare,
    down to its foundations!'

And in Lamentations 4:21 there is a bitter and ironic invitation to the Edomites to rejoice, followed by a declaration of judgement:

Rejoice and be glad, O daughter of Edom,
    you who dwell in the land of Uz;
but to you also the cup shall pass;
    you shall become drunk and strip yourself bare.
The punishment of your iniquity, O daughter of Zion, is accomplished;
    he will keep you in exile no longer;
but your iniquity, O daughter of Edom, he will punish;
    he will uncover your sins.

DO NOT BOAST

Literally this means 'and do not make great with your mouth'. Do not be a big mouth; do not talk big. Ezekiel's oracle (35:12–15) relates to this:

I have heard all the revilings that you uttered against the mountains of Israel, saying, 'They are laid desolate; they are given us to devour.' And you magnified yourselves against me with your mouth, and multiplied your words against me; I heard it. Thus says the Lord GOD: While the whole earth rejoices, I will make you desolate. As you rejoiced over the inheritance of the house of Israel, because it was desolate, so I will deal with you; you shall be desolate, Mount Seir, and all Edom, all of it. Then they will know that I am the LORD.

On verse 12 as a whole, Calvin comments:

It is a feeling naturally implanted in us, that when one is distressed, we are touched with pity; even when we see our enemies lie prostrate on the ground, our hatred and anger are extinguished, or at least are abated: and all who see even their enemies ill-treated, become, as it were, other men, that is, they put off the anger with which they were previously inflamed. As then this is what is common almost to all men, it appears that the Idumaeans must have been doubly and trebly barbarous, when they rejoiced at the calamity of their brethren, and took pleasure in a spectacle so sad and mournful.[10]

DO NOT ENTER THE GATE OF MY PEOPLE

The sins of the Edomites were compounded. Having stood by and then drawn close to look and to laugh, they then entered the city itself, gloated further and got involved in looting and plundering the possessions of God's people. Entering the gates is, as we have already seen in verse 11, the action of an enemy, not a brother. The gates of a city represented its security and integrity, and since, in the Bible, the city is often portrayed as a woman, a forced entrance by hostile troops amounts to a type of rape violation. Once this has happened, the virgin city has fallen (see Ezek. 26:10; Ps. 87:2; Lam. 4:12–13).

God does not call Jerusalem his daughter here, though it is astonishing that he still calls the judged, humiliated and defeated Jews 'my people'— and does so while addressing the Edomites in their hearing. This itself is a comfort for the Jews, a reminder of their underlying identity, and a threat to the Edomites, who have touched the apple of God's eye.

Putting these things together (that invasion is violation, cities are women and God still calls the Jews 'my people'), the disgusting wickedness of the Edomites is clearly seen and the intensity of God's anger understandable. The invasion and destruction of Jerusalem (considered just from the perspective of the sinful actions of those responsible and not from the perspective of the righteous judgement upon Judah which it represented) can be summed up in four of the most chilling, bitter, furious and threatening words that any man can say: 'You raped my daughter.'

DO NOT LAY HOLD OF / STRETCH OUT HIS FORCE / SUBSTANCE

This is rendered 'do not loot his wealth' in the ESV. Some commentators think that the text should read 'send your hand'. Whether or not they are right, the meaning is certainly along these lines, which is why it is translated in ways such as 'lay hold of', 'reach out for' and so on.[11]

DO NOT STAND AT THE CROSSROADS

Coming to verse 14, we reach the callous and cruel climax of the Edomites' nastiness. The overall sense is clear: the Edomites stood in places where they could cut off Jews who were trying to escape being taking into exile; they then handed those they caught over to the Babylonians (see Deut. 23:15; 32:30; 1 Sam. 23:11; 2 Kings 25:3–7 for similar actions).

TO CUT OFF HIS FUGITIVES

'Cut off' could mean 'kill' or possibly 'catch' (the same word has already been used in vv. 9–10), but it makes more sense to read it as 'catch' or 'intercept'—it would be odd to 'kill' in verse 14b and then 'hand over' in 14c. Once again, the fact that the same word that was used in verses 9–10 is used here underlines the appropriateness of God's judgement. The Edomites 'cut off' the Jews, and so God will 'cut off' the Edomites. 'Fugitives' are those surviving and fleeing war or judgement (see also Gen. 14:13; Josh. 8:22; Judg. 12:4–5; Isa. 66:19; Jer. 42:17; Lam. 2:22; Amos 9:1). Verse 17 will take this word up: the Edomites intended that there should be none who escaped, yet God will make sure that there is 'escape' on Mount Zion.

DO NOT HAND OVER [DELIVER UP] HIS SURVIVORS

The word translated 'survivors' or 'what is left, the remnant' is different from the 'fugitives' word of the previous line. Verse 18 will take up this word: the Edomites intended that there should be no survivors among the Jews, and God will ensure that there are no survivors among the Edomites (see Num. 21:35; Deut. 2:34; Josh. 8:22; 10:33; Isa. 1:9; Jer. 42:17; Lam. 2:22).

Study questions

1. Edom's sins in these verses can be summarized as:
- showing indifference towards the suffering of God's people;
- feeling pleasure in the suffering of God's people;
- taking no action during the suffering of God's people;
- contributing to the suffering of God's people.

Contrast this with descriptions of brotherly love found in Matthew 25:31–46; Romans 12:15; 1 Corinthians 12:26; 13:4–6; 2 Corinthians 8–9; James 2:14–17; 1 Peter 1:22–2:1; 1 John 3:11–18.

2. What are the different sorts of violence that break the second great command, 'Love your neighbour as yourself'?

3. Trace some of the ways in which the Bible uses the image of people being clothed—in shame, beauty, glory, strength, righteousness and so on.

4. How might it be said of you, 'You were like one of them' (v. 11e)? Look at the company Peter keeps and the words he speaks at the charcoal fire in John 18:18,25 (contrast them with his company and words at the charcoal fire in John 21:9) and think through the question in terms of 'With whom do you stand, warming yourself?'

5. Are there ways in which you could come to the relief of God's suffering people right now?

6. Taking a cue from the 'rhetoric' of verses 12–14, how important is it for us to 'inhabit' the scene of suffering and evil in order to fully feel godly outrage at wickedness and godly compassion for the suffering? How can we use our imaginations so that we can 'be there' with the persecuted church?

7. Meditate successively upon the distressed words of verses 12–14 with the persecuted church or suffering believers whom you know in mind.

8. What are the implications of God still calling his defeated, humiliated people 'my people' when they are at their weakest?

Notes

1 **Hans Walter Wolff,** *Obadiah and Jonah: A Commentary* (Minneapolis: Augsburg Publishing House, 1986). Comment on vv. 11–14.

2 'Capturing' or 'carrying off' happens to both people and goods. See, for example, 1 Chr. 5:21; 2 Chr. 14:14–15; 21:17.

3 **Jeffrey Niehaus,** 'Obadiah', in **Thomas E. McComiskey** (ed.), *The Minor Prophets*, vol. ii (Grand Rapids, MI: Baker, 1993). Comment on v. 11.

4 This idea comes from **Ehud Ben Zvi,** 'A Historical–Critical Study of the Book of Obadiah', in *Beihefte zur ZAW,* 242(1996), p. 256.

5 **Leslie Allen,** *Joel, Obadiah, Jonah and Micah* (NICOT; Grand Rapids, MI: Eerdmans, 1976), p. 156. Similar comments are found in **Irvin A. Busenitz,** *Joel and Obadiah* (Mentor Commentary; Fearn: Christian Focus, 2003) and in the NET Bible notes at http://www.bible.org/netbible/index.htm.

6 As we have noted before, the pronouns vary ('his' and 'their'). The Hebrew word for 'calamity' that is used three times in verse 13 is probably a play on words because it sounds rather like 'Edom'—this was the day of Judah's 'edom'. The first word, 'misfortune', is, in the Hebrew, like the word translated 'strangers' in verse 11: it was a day of alienation or estrangement. The word for 'destruction' or 'ruin' in verse 12 is the word used for the destruction of the wise men in verse 8. The word for 'distress', which occurs in verses 12 and 14, is used elsewhere for a range of trouble, adversity and tribulation—Gen. 35:3; Judg. 10:14; 1 Sam. 26:24; 2 Sam. 4:9; Job 5:19; Ps. 9:9; 20:1; 46:1; Prov. 17:17; 25:19; Isa. 46:7; Jer. 14:8; Nahum 1:7.

7 **Thomas Finley,** *Joel, Amos, Obadiah* (Wycliffe Exegetical Commentary; Chicago: Moody Press, 1990). Comments on vv. 12–14.

8 **John Trapp,** *A Commentary or Exposition upon the XII Minor Prophets* (London, 1654). Comment on vv. 13–14.

9 **Matthew Henry,** *A Commentary upon the Whole Bible*, vol. iv (1712; [n.d.], Iowa Falls, IA: World Bible Publishers), p. 1274.

10 **John Calvin,** *Commentaries upon the Twelve Minor Prophets*, vol. ii: *Joel, Amos, Obadiah,* trans. John Owen (Edinburgh: Calvin Translation Society, 1846), Lecture LXXI, p. 442.

11 If the word 'hand' should be in the text as such then it would be parallel to its use in Exod. 22:7; 1 Sam. 24:6; Esth. 2:21; 9:10. The word which I have translated as 'substance' here also appears in v. 11. In both instances, the ESV gives 'wealth'.

Jesus in Obadiah (1): the Master story (vv. 10–14)

I wonder whether God has a favourite shape. Lots of candidates come to mind, but the shape of a tick or a hockey stick must be close to the top of the list. This is because the tick shape is God's preferred way of doing things. It is, after all, the basic shape of a story, and God loves telling stories.

For a story, we need:

- A starting point (the top left of the tick). 'Once upon a time there was a little girl called Red Riding Hood.' This is the situation in which things are good.
- A problem (the descending left line of the tick). 'So the wolf gobbled up Red Riding Hood as well as her Granny.' The situation is bad; this might be because of an external enemy, a distance to be travelled, a treasure to be found, an immaturity to be overcome or an obstacle to true love to be removed.
- A solution (the turn at the bottom of the tick). 'The woodsman killed the wolf while he slept, cut him open and out climbed Red Riding Hood and her Granny, a little crumpled but otherwise well.' There has been a saving intervention to put things straight.
- An ending (the top right of the tick). 'They had a fine tea together and they all lived happily ever after.' At the end, things are even better than they were at the beginning. The threat has been removed, the dragon slain or the treasure found. The lovers marry, the celebration is held and 'they all lived happily ever after'.

The shape of the story is clear, isn't it? Good to bad to better than ever:

- Starting point—good

- Problem (distance, descent, darkness, death)—bad
- Intervention (victory, reconciliation, restoration, return, renewal or resurrection)—the turning point
- Ending (joy, light, love, order, beauty)—better than ever

This happens again and again in the Bible.

Adam starts in a good place but then descends into the 'death' and darkness of a deep sleep, during which he is torn apart to give life to the bride whom he meets on awaking. Good to bad to better than ever.

Joseph is in a good place but is then sold, betrayed, imprisoned and forgotten before God raises him up to rule the land and restore his family. Good to bad to better than ever.

The Hebrews start in a good place but then go down into oppression and slavery in Egypt, from which God brings them up and out and into the promised land. Good to bad to better than ever.

David. Job. Jonah. Daniel. Peter. Psalm 73. Psalm 107. Whenever in the Bible you see a valley, darkness, exile, death, a curse, imprisonment or lostness, then you know that you are at the bottom of the tick.

But why are stories like this, and why does God cause this pattern to be played out repeatedly in history?

The answer, as to all Sunday school questions, is 'Jesus'. His is the 'Master' story, and all others are 'servant' stories. If, for a story, you need information, time and goal, then it is clear that the Lord Jesus Christ, in whom are hidden all the treasures of wisdom and knowledge (information!), who is before all things, the first and the last (time!), and who is the heir of all things and the one for whom all things were created (goal!), is himself the focus and Lord of story. He is *the* Story.

Now, every time the Father speaks, the word that comes out is his Son. Every time the Spirit blows, the whisper in that wind is Jesus. God thunders the name of his beloved One so loudly that it echoes off every person, object and event in the universe. So, if the one great story of Jesus the King is the Master story, then all the stories we find in God's Word and God's world will, deliberately and inescapably, point to Jesus. God is a God of pattern and habit, and since the greatest thing that he does in the history of the world is the tick-shaped redemption of humankind and the cosmos in the life, death and resurrection of the Lord Jesus Christ, he puts this pattern everywhere in the lives of individuals and groups, in the patterns of nature, and in the elemental structure of a story.

God so loves his Son and is so determined that all shall honour the Son that, again and again in history and then recorded again and again in Scripture, God plays out dress rehearsals for the Great Drama, he tries out pencil sketches for the Masterpiece in Oils and he produces theme-line melodies which will be played out and transfigured in the Glorious Symphony that is coming in the Lord Jesus Christ.

So, whether we are talking about a thousand and one tales or just about seven basic plots,[1] they are all related to the one great Master story, which is the tick-shaped story of darkness to light, the punishment of the wicked and the vindication of the oppressed. It is the 'good-to-bad-to-better-than-ever' story, which ends with the enemy defeated and return home, the restoration of order, the possession of inheritance, the exercise of righteous rule and the manifestation and celebration of the glory of God. This is the story of Jesus and, by means of it, we are ready to see another way in which Obadiah points us to Christ.

What, then, is the *story* of Obadiah? Can a prophecy tell a story? Yes, of course: a prophecy is spoken to particular people who have done or suffered certain things, in order to pass judgement, for good or ill, upon those things. A prophecy stands between events which have already happened and actions which have already been performed on the one hand, and events which are yet to take place and actions which are yet to be performed on the other hand. And those events and actions, past and future, amount to a story.

The *story* of Obadiah, then, is that the Edomites behaved as enemies of God's people at the fall of Jerusalem, although they should have behaved as brothers. As a result, they would be punished by God as part of his intervention to bring justice and order to the whole world. Conversely, the Jews, who at the time of the prophecy were a defeated and dispossessed people, would be rescued, returned home and brought into full possession and enjoyment of their inheritance, ruling over their former enemies. God's kingship would be established, demonstrated and experienced.

This is to say that Obadiah, just like every other tick-shaped story of the Old Testament, is one of those rehearsals, pencil sketches or theme-line melodies we mentioned earlier; if we spend a little time meditating on parts of Obadiah, we will see this.

The form that the 'basic plot' takes in Obadiah is that God's own is first insulted and defeated, mocked, beaten and humiliated. Then God's own is vindicated and rescued, restored and given possession and rule.

God's own is defeated and humiliated (vv. 10–14)

What happens to God's people in these verses does not *predict* what would happen to Jesus but it does *make us think about* what would happen to Jesus. We are not surprised to see this; just as Herod the Idumaean (Edomite) failed to recognize and delight in the Lord Jesus but rather joined with the outsiders (Romans) in condemning and humiliating him (see Mark 3:6 and Luke 23:6–12), so, back in Obadiah, we see the Edomites failing to sympathize with and support the Jews but rather joining with the outsiders (Babylonians) to condemn and humiliate them. The Edomites join in; they plot, mock and plunder; they line up with the enemies of God's own.

VERSE 10

Just as the Jews suffered violence from those who should have known and done better, and just as 'Jacob's' own brother had done violence to him, so the Lord Jesus Christ came to his own and his own did not receive him. He, too, suffered violence from the very people who should have recognized him as God's Son.

VERSE 11

As God's people were plundered and their possessions divided up by lot, those who should have helped—or, at the least, sympathized—looked on with the attitude of the enemies themselves. And as the Romans desecrated the holy place of the body of Jesus and cast lots for his garments, so the Jewish leaders—those who should have welcomed Jesus as Messiah and submitted to him—stood by and watched with pleasure as he was humiliated.

VERSE 12

This was the day of Jerusalem's calamity and distress, yet it was also a day when the wails of God's people were mingled with the shrieks of callous delight from the onlooking Edomites. They mocked, gloated and boasted over God's own. We are reminded of how much of the Gospel accounts of the trial and death of the Lord Jesus is taken up with the mocking and boasting of his enemies. The soldiers stripped him, they robed him in emperor's clothes, they knelt before him and pretended to honour him. They struck him, spat on him and asked the blindfolded Jesus, 'Who hit you?' The crowds, the authorities, the priests and those crucified with Jesus all took part in the humiliating mockery of that day.

VERSE 13

Just as the Edomites entered the city and looted its wealth, so the Lord Jesus Christ, the City of True Humanity, was invaded and despoiled.

VERSE 14

The Jews went into exile and, even as they did so, were killed or handed over to the darkness. So on the cross, the Lord Jesus was in exile—

banished under the curse of God to the far country of alienation, darkness and judgement.

So we see that the first half of the *story* of Obadiah takes us to Christ through the betrayal and defeat of God's own mocked, stripped of its possessions and dignity, destroyed, exiled and humiliated. We take Obadiah's outrage and anguish at the ruin and distress that came upon the Jews and, gazing at the violation of God's own on the cross of Jesus, we feel similar outrage and anguish.

God's own is vindicated and restored (vv. 17–21)

VERSE 17

The defeated and crushed people of God find that, through his kind, just and powerful intervention, they are rescued. There is escape and survival in Mount Zion, the place where God dwells and makes himself known. There is a future when it seems that all hope has gone. Meditating on this, we find ourselves outside the empty tomb on Easter Sunday morning. God has intervened in kindness, justice and power to deliver Jesus from the power of death, the grip of the grave. God has stepped in in holy might to rescue his dear Son from destruction. The resurrection of Jesus is the deliverance of God's own. And in the resurrection he is 'set apart' as the Son of God in power (Rom. 1:3–4) to be close to God, both in the sense of *near* God (at his right hand, in fact) and in the sense of *like* God.

The deliverance which God gives to his people, in view of their previous humiliation, can only be seen as a vindication, a pronouncement from God that, yes, these are *his* people. And this is exactly what we see in the resurrection of the Lord Jesus Christ. That resurrection, that deliverance from death, is God's vindication of his Son. The resurrection is God's verdict over Jesus: 'I am perfectly satisfied with you.' In that sense it is the 'justification' of Jesus—the judicial declaration that Jesus is God's righteous Son. The wonderful news of the gospel is that the judicial verdict, 'perfectly satisfied', which God declared over Jesus in the resurrection, is thereby also declared over every single person who, by faith, is joined to or is in union with Jesus.

VERSES 18–20

God's rescued, restored, vindicated and set-apart people enter into full possession of their inheritance and are granted authority to own and rule all the land which God has promised them, enjoying it and living in it with God as King over them. When we meditate on these verses in the light of the fact that the story of Obadiah is serving the Master story of the Lord Jesus Christ, we cannot but think of the enthronement and present rule of Christ. The Father has placed all things into his hands. All authority in heaven and on earth has been given to Christ. Jesus asks the Father and receives the nations for his inheritance, the ends of the earth for his possession. He is to have first place in everything. He is the Heir of all things. He is Ruler of the kings of the earth. He is the Meek who shall inherit the earth. He is the obedient Son who will live long in the land. He is the Seed of Abraham who inherits the world. And this takes place at the resurrection, ascension and enthronement of Jesus.

Obadiah, then, takes us to the Lord Jesus Christ by being the 'servant' story pointing to the Master story. The story of Obadiah is that God's own is betrayed, humiliated, defeated, crushed, mocked and exiled; and then that God's own is delivered, restored, vindicated, set apart, given possession, triumph and rule, taking over the world under the kingship of God, surrounded by the mocking of those who should have known better, restored to enter the inheritance promised by God. When we read that story, there is no doubt where the Spirit intends us to go. We cannot but think about the Lord Jesus Christ. The pattern, the structure, the shape and the story of Obadiah point to, are played out in and are expanded by the real 'God's own', Jesus Christ.

It might be asked, 'Why would we do this? Haven't we got Matthew 26–27, Mark 14–15 and so on? What is the point of meditating on the death and resurrection of Jesus from Obadiah when we have whole sections of the New Testament explicitly about these things?' The answer can be given briefly: because we love Christ and we would go anywhere to see him. He is our hope, our hero and our joy. Yes, we'll be there on Saturday afternoon to see the world's greatest footballer in Premiership action. But if you tell us that we can watch him on the training ground on a wet Wednesday, then we'll be there too. Yes, we'll be there on Saturday night at Covent Garden to hear the world's greatest soprano sing. But if you tell us that she is doing her voice exercises first thing tomorrow morning, then we'll be up early to attend and to listen.

We meditate on Christ through the story of Obadiah because the Father speaks of his Son that way and we want to attend to everything the Father tells us about the Son. Every angle tells us something new—and if we have to look more closely, think more carefully and ponder more deeply, this will be a good thing. And the adumbration of the great story of Jesus the King which we find in Obadiah will make us fans of Obadiah for the rest of our lives.

Gerard Manley Hopkins invites us to see Christ everywhere:

For Christ plays in ten thousand places,
lovely in limbs and lovely in eyes not his
to the Father, through the features of men's faces.[2]

And since the same Spirit who loves to testify of Christ, to take of the things of Christ and make them known to us and to glorify Christ is the one who caused Obadiah to be written with the exact structure and shape that it has, then we should be unsurprised to find—and utterly committed to finding more and more deeply—that a faithful reading of this little book of the Old Testament is a sure and delightful way of meeting our Lord Jesus afresh.

Study questions

1. See the 'seven basic plots' in this chapter's endnote and describe the story of God's work of salvation through Jesus by means of each of them. How is the gospel a story of each of these:

- overcoming the monster
- rags to riches
- journey and return
- the quest (for treasure, to destroy the Ring, etc.)
- comedy (an obstacle to the lover's union is removed and all ends happily)
- tragedy (the strong turns evil and must end up dead)
- rebirth?

2. Philippians 3:9–10 shows us that the 'shape' of Jesus's story (death and resurrection) is played out in the lives of his people. In what ways do we see and experience, individually and together as the church of Jesus Christ, the 'humiliation deaths' of Obadiah 10–14 and the 'vindication resurrections' of Obadiah 17–21?

Notes

1 **Christopher Booker** gives the following: Overcoming the Monster; Rags to Riches; Journey and Return; The Quest; Comedy; Tragedy; Rebirth. It is a fascinating and rewarding exercise to see how God's great work of salvation can be described according to each of these basic plots (*The Seven Basic Plots* (London: Continuum, 2004)).

2 **Gerard Manley Hopkins,** 'As Kingfishers Catch Fire', in **W.H. Gardner** and **N.H. Mackenzie** (eds.), *The Poems of Gerard Manley Hopkins,* 4th edn. (Oxford: OUP, 1970), p. 90.

Jesus in Obadiah (2): faith, hope and love (vv. 10–14)

We have looked at one way in which the book of Obadiah points us to God's work in and through the Lord Jesus Christ, namely, by means of the overall 'shape' of the 'story'. Later, in Chapters 9 and 10, we will see how the ways in which the New Testament picks up on the actual prophecies of Obadiah show that these prophecies are fulfilled in and through Christ. We will also see how, when we draw a picture of the world as it would be if Obadiah's vision were realized, we find that the Lord Jesus Christ is the only one who can establish such a world; that he has, in fact, done so; and that he stands at the centre of it.

In this chapter, we will again be considering how Obadiah points us to the Lord Jesus Christ. It is impossible not to notice that at the heart of Obadiah's prophecy is God's denunciation of the Edomites. And although verses 10–14 give us the description of those sins and crimes for which they were especially coming under judgement, other sins are implied elsewhere in the prophecy. But every time we see descriptions and denunciations of sin in the Bible, we are reminded that in his life, the Lord Jesus embodied the opposite of these sins; that in his death, the Lord Jesus bore the punishment for these sins; and that in his resurrection power, the Lord Jesus intends to purge these sins from the lives of his disciples. In this way, we are able to take every single passage of Scripture about sin as an opportunity to think about Jesus.

In particular, the sins of Edom can be regarded as failures of faith, hope and love:

- a failure of faith seen in the pride of verses 2–4—they do not see things God's way.

- a failure of hope seen in the false reliances of verses 5–9—they put their trust in things that cannot deliver.
- a failure of love seen in the uncharitableness of verses 10–14—they seek the harm, not the good, of others.

And, to restate what was said above, we see Christ through a consideration of these sins in three ways:

- In his perfect humanness and his complete obedience to the lovely law of God, the Lord Jesus lived the opposite of these sins: in verses 2–4, the Edomites are proud and therefore humbled; he is humble and therefore exalted; in verses 5–9, they are idolatrous and their false gods fail; he dependently walks God's path and his way prospers; in verses 10–14, they are uncharitable and seek the harm of others; he is love and seeks the good of others.
- Since these are sins of which we too are guilty, we know that, when Christ was made sin for us, when he bore the curse, was torn apart for sin and bore the penalty for sin, then God's righteous anger against these very sins in his people fell upon Christ.
- Since God's intention is to bring each of his people to the likeness of the Lord Jesus, he is, by the Spirit's work, purging these sins from us now.

Thus we see the opposite of these sins *in* Jesus; we see the punishment of these sins *on* Jesus; we experience deliverance from these sins *through* Jesus. In the life of Jesus, we see the pattern of life which contradicts these sins; through the death of Jesus, we experience the pardon which we need for having committed these sins ourselves; in the resurrection of Jesus and through his Spirit's work, we receive the power to say 'no' to these sins and be conformed to the likeness of Christ.

God hated these sins in Edom, punished these sins in Jesus and purges these sins from his people.

Pride: a failure of faith, not seeing things God's way (vv. 2–4)

Pride is associated in the Bible with 'high' and 'low'. In their pride, the

Edomites placed themselves 'high'. They set their seat in the heights. It is common in Scripture for matters of pride to be described in these ways. A look at Isaiah 2:9–13 shows this. And there is the famous king of Babylon from Isaiah 14, whose pride and humbling are described as follows:

How you are fallen from heaven,
O Day Star, son of Dawn!
How you are cut down to the ground,
you who laid the nations low!
You said in your heart,
'I will ascend to heaven;
above the stars of God
I will set my throne on high;
I will sit on the mount of assembly
in the far reaches of the north;
I will ascend above the heights of the clouds;
I will make myself like the Most High.'
But you are brought down to Sheol,
to the far reaches of the pit.

The proud man in the parable is humbled and goes with shame to the 'lowest place', whereas the humble is told, 'Friend, move up higher' (Luke 14:7–11). That section ends with Jesus' statement which he repeats elsewhere: 'For everyone who exalts himself will be humbled, and he who humbles himself will be exalted.'

Pride deceives people. It is, in itself, an inaccurate view of the world, and it leads to other errors, too. Here the Edomites' pride deceives them with regard to their security—they think that they are safer than they actually are.

Pride may be a secret thing, yet God knows it. It is the pride of the Edomites' hearts which leads them to say things in their hearts. But God knows what human beings say in their hearts, and even the most carefully concealed proud thought is known to him.

Pride often leads to boasting. Here the Edomites boast, by means of a proud question, that no one will be able to bring them down (v. 3); as we noticed before, this is a challenge which God takes up! After all, human beings are to glory or boast in the Lord and not in their own wisdom, strength or achievements. When they boast in themselves rather than in God, this is simultaneously a form of blasphemy (speaking ill of God by failing to render him the praise which he is due) and of idolatry (giving to things or persons other than God the praise which is rightly his and thereby putting other things before God).

The key moment in human history when humans proudly placed themselves too 'high' was in the garden of Eden when Adam, tempted by the serpent, aimed to make himself equal with God. He had been made the pinnacle of creation by God (Ps. 8) but was not content with this and, in reaching up to the heights of divinity, he overstretched and came crashing down from his high place. He had 'fallen' into the pit of sin, death and condemnation.

Thousands of years later, a second Adam came into the world. He was in the form of God, equal with God, but he did not consider equality with God something to be exploited or clung on to. Whereas in pride the first Adam had disobeyed and fallen from high to low, the second Adam, the Lord Jesus Christ, in humility obeyed God and made himself low. He came down to the pit of sin, death and condemnation where the first Adam lay helpless. And, because he was obedient—even to the death of the cross—God raised him to the highest heights, above all rule, authority, dominion and power. The wonder of the gospel is that all who by faith are connected to the Lord Jesus Christ are raised together with him, up from the pit of sin, death and condemnation, to be seated with Christ in the heavenly realms and to share his life. (See Phil. 2:5–11 and Eph. 1:19–2:10 for these ways of understanding the gospel.)

Thus the call comes to Christians to walk the way of the Lord Jesus, which is the way of humility.

Idolatry: a failure of hope, placing trust in the wrong things (vv. 5–9)

Idolatry is the worship of any person, thing, idea, ideal or force which is not the true God. It is to place ultimate hope in anything created rather than in the one God who is the uncreated Creator of all things.

All human beings realize that the world is not perfect and that things could be better. One of the key questions that can be asked to discover a person's worldview (way of understanding the world) is 'What's wrong with the world?' or 'How could the world be made better?' Put more fully, the question could be phrased, 'What is necessary to bring human wholeness, security, prosperity and maturity?' or 'How could we see the world put back together in the way that it ought to be?'

The answers to these questions amount to a person's 'religion', 'gospel' or 'god', no matter how much that person may protest that he or she is not religious or does not believe in a god. More simply still, we could ask for the following two sentences to be completed:

* Things would be OK if …
* Things will be OK because …

Had the Edomites been asked such questions, it is clear what their answers would have been. Things would be OK if they were allowed to enjoy the plunder they had stolen from Jerusalem and continue the pleasure which resulted from seeing the Jews suffer. And things would be OK because they were wealthy, they had strong allies, they were wise and they had great military might combined with virtually impregnable rocky strongholds. They were trusting in their own possessions and attributes.

All sorts of other answers might be given to these questions today. Things would be OK if we had a better education system, greater economic growth, a change of government or perhaps more of the same government.

Things would be OK if we had more fluoride in the water, less fluoride in the water, if we brought back hanging, reintroduced national service, provided better living conditions for people, could see further scientific progress, if we just had more time, better family life, less advertising, more respect for others, if we got rid of religion … and on and on.

Every one of these is a false gospel. No matter how good some of those things might be in themselves, if they are relied upon as the way to sort out people's problems and bring human beings to wholeness, they are false gods, false gospels.

The Lord Jesus Christ alone shows us how the world is put back together. In the wilderness, when he was tempted, he refused all false trails, all Satanic alternatives, all idolatrous methods of making 'progress' (Luke 4:1–13). At Caesarea Philippi, he again denounced the easy short cuts represented by Peter's opposition to the way of the cross (Mark 8:31–33). And in the garden of Gethsemane, on the night before he was crucified, he again acknowledged that his Father's way was best (Mark 14:32–36). Submission to the perfect ways of God, worship of God alone, living on his Word and walking his paths, even to the cross, was how the Lord Jesus himself won forgiveness and renewal for his vast people.

And as the Spirit works in the people of God to purge them of the sins of the Edomites and all others and to work in them the character and mind of the Lord Jesus Christ, so all false hopes, false gods and false gospels must be demolished and must give way to humble, obedient, trusting reliance on God and his ways alone. For individuals or local churches or nations to place their hope in wealth, allies, wisdom or military might is for them to be aligned with Edom. And those who are aligned with Edom in its sin will be aligned with Edom in its punishment.

Uncharitableness: a failure of love, seeking the harm, not the good, of others (vv. 10–14)

If the sin of idolatry, seen in verses 5–9, is the transgression of the first great commandment (to love the Lord our God with the whole of our being), then the sin of uncharitableness, which lies at the heart of the book of Obadiah, is the transgression of the second great commandment—to love our neighbours as ourselves.

In verse 10, the Edomites have sinned against the obligation to support their brothers, the Jews. In verse 11, we see them siding with the strong, avoiding demanding situations, keeping out of the way and doing nothing, even when their neighbours were suffering. In verse 12, it goes further—pleasure in the suffering of others. And in verses 13–14, the trespass, contempt, theft, treachery and vindictiveness all heaped up Edom's guilt.

All of these attitudes and actions were failures of love. Love means seeking and working for the good of the other. It means giving oneself to bless and enrich the other. But the Edomite way was a life organized around and turned in on the self. It was the opposite of the way of God, whose very life as triune is other-person centred.

When we look at ourselves as sinners, we see the Edomite in ourselves. Indifferent to the pain of others, sometimes even rejoicing in the pain of others, and, worse, even contributing to the pain of others, there is something drastically, deeply, radically twisted in us. Secretly and profoundly, we do *not* want the well-being of other people. What foul sort of animal is a human being, what demonic thing can a person be, that, faced with other persons, does not want their well-being but is indifferent to, pleased by or even adds to their distress? What wicked idiocy is it in me that thinks that the happiness or well-being of another human being hurts me or that their distress enriches me?

Twelve 'destroyers' have their home in our hearts:
- seven deadly sins: pride, covetousness, lust, envy, gluttony, rage, sloth
- three false reactions: fear, guilt, anger
- two end-of-the-line evils: boredom, malice

From these proceed all forms and degrees of lovelessness, all failures to live the way of the Lord Jesus Christ as described in 1 Corinthians 13:4–7. Suddenly the words of Titus 3:3 no longer seem overstated: 'For we ourselves were once foolish, disobedient, led astray, slaves to various passions and pleasures, passing our days in malice and envy, hated by others and hating one another.' This is life as an Edomite, life as a sinner. It is mean and squalid and hateful.

And now the beauty of a life of real love is all the more attractive. What if there were someone who lived the opposite of Obadiah 10–14? What if there were someone who was not indifferent to the distress of others but who really cared? What if he gave himself to deal with that distress? What if there were someone who did not just stand there watching but came to the place of sin and suffering and wept, who went to the place of wickedness and condemnation and died? That would be amazing.

What if there were someone who took upon himself the crushing, cursing punishment my filth deserves? One who knew none of this sin but was made this sin for us, who bore the wrath we call down on ourselves by living this way? Who embodied and enacted 1 Corinthians 13:4–7— who was patient and kind, who did not envy or boast, who was not arrogant or rude and who did not insist on his own way? Someone who was not irritable or resentful, did not rejoice at wrongdoing but rejoiced with the truth, who bore all things, believed all things, hoped all things and endured all things? That would be no Edomite false brother, that would be a Saviour true brother.

And what if his resurrection life were strong enough by the power of the Spirit to change us, to rid us of the unloving selfishness by which we have lived and to plant his own love inside us to work itself out in lives of self-forgetful service of others and to continue to grow every day of our lives?

If there were such a one, we would love him. We would throw ourselves on him for mercy and give ourselves to him for the rest of our lives. We would spend our lives under his authority and for all eternity praise him.

There is such a one. We know his name. And consideration of the sins of the Edomites in Obadiah verses 10–14 has brought us to his feet. God be praised.

Study questions

1. Consider the three great sins of pride, idolatry and uncharitableness as they are presented elsewhere in the Bible and contrast them with faith, hope and love as *they* are presented elsewhere in the Bible.

2. Discuss the threefold way of allowing passages about sin to lead us to consider the Lord Jesus Christ: that he lived the opposite of this sin, he died to bear the penalty of this sin in his people, he intends to purge his people of this sin. Is this a helpful way of reading such passages?

International justice (vv. 15–16)

In verses 2–4, God took up Edom's proud challenge, 'Who will bring me down?' and declared that he, God, would do just that, humiliating Edom and causing it to be despised. In verses 5–9, God stated that the coming judgement of Edom would be a complete judgement and one that Edom's allies, wisdom or military strength would be unable to avert. In verses 10–14, the sin of Edom was vividly described, bringing home the utter wickedness of Edom's attitudes and actions at the time when, in 587 BC, the Babylonians defeated Jerusalem and destroyed the temple.

Still, however, the people of God, hearing (as God intended they should) what God has said to the Edomites, might be asking, 'How can we *know* that this is going to happen? It all seems so unlikely. We Jewish exiles are the humiliated ones; what assurance do we have that the Edomites, who at the moment seem so pleased with themselves and so secure, will really be judged? How can we *know* that God really is going to step in like this?'

In verses 15–16, God, still formally speaking to the Edomites (although really with the intention that his people should hear), gives that reassurance that the judgement of Edom will take place. He grounds this reassurance upon the announcement that he will decisively step into history to put things straight, that is, that the 'day of the LORD' is near. The judgement of Edom is part of God's intervention to put the world right.

(v. 15a) For the day of the LORD is near upon all the nations.
(v. 15b) As you have done, it shall be done to you;
(v. 15c) your deeds shall return on your own head.
(v. 16a) For as you have drunk on my holy mountain,

(v. 16*b*) *so all the nations shall drink continually;*

(v. 16*c*) *they shall drink and swallow,*

(v. 16*d*) *and shall be as though they had never been.*

These verses have often been misunderstood, and some commentators have even wanted to rearrange the order of some of the phrases in them because of two unwarranted assumptions that have been brought to the text rather than found in it:

- Some readers have assumed that the phrase 'the day of the LORD' can only refer to the glorious return of Jesus to judge the world at the end of history. Because of this assumption, they have confused themselves and others about the character and timing of the judgement of Edom.
- Some readers have assumed that the reference to 'drinking' must relate to the important and common biblical idea of 'drinking the cup/wine of God's wrath'. Because of this assumption, they have confused themselves and others about who is being addressed in 16*a*.

These assumptions lead to a reading which runs like this:

As you Edomites have done, so it shall be done to you; your deeds shall return on your own head. And not just Edomites, but all nations—the day of the LORD is close. As you Jews have drunk the cup of my wrath at the time of the destruction of the temple, so all the nations will drink of my wrath and be destroyed.

But, setting aside these unwarranted assumptions, the verses are better read like this:

So, Edom, we're on the verge of (another of) God's international payback interventions, so there is no way that you are going to escape judgement. As you have done, so it shall be done to you—all your sins shall be punished. And just as you drank in mad and wicked revelry at the fall of Jerusalem, so when I step in again to set things right I will force all the nations to keep drinking and drinking and drinking until they collapse in their own wickedness and stupor, unable to rise. Do you really think, Edom, that you can escape? No way.

The arguments, one way and another, about why the 'you' of 16*a* should still refer to the Edomites rather than shifting suddenly to the Jews are complicated and can be seen in Appendix 1. The main point is that these verses do not represent a change of subject but are rather the climax and confirmation of God's threat upon Edom. Edom getting what it deserves is part of God's dealings with the nations. The point is not, 'And, moving further afield, what has happened to Edom will happen to the nations', but rather, 'And, because of God's international interventions, the preceding threats against Edom are absolutely certain'.[1]

FOR THE DAY OF THE LORD IS NEAR

We have already seen that the book of Obadiah is a book about two 'days'. The first was the 'day' of Edom's sin. The second, mentioned in verse 8 and now described in more detail, is the 'day' of the LORD. The first was the day of distress for the people of God, but the second, the LORD's day, will be the day of distress for Edom.

'The day of the LORD' is a phrase which occurs directly sixteen times in the Old Testament prophets (Isa. 13:6,9; Ezek. 13:5; Joel 1:15; 2:1,11,31; 3:14; Amos 5:18*a–b*,20 Obad. 15; Zeph. 1:7,14*a–b*; Mal. 4:5). Additionally, there are other closely related references (Isa. 2:12; 22:5; 34:8; Zech. 14:1; Jer. 46:10; Zeph. 1:8; Ezek. 7:19; Zeph. 1:18; 2:2–3; Lam. 2:22).

We have a tendency to overemphasize the 'the' in the phrase, as if there can only ever be one 'day of the LORD'. But in the Old Testament references, the 'day of the LORD' is usually spoken of as future and, often, near. The fall of Jerusalem in 587 BC was 'the day of the anger of the LORD'. And the same event was 'the day of the LORD' which Ezekiel prophesied in 7:19 and 30:3. The 'day of the LORD' which Amos announced presumably came with the fall of the northern kingdom in 722 BC (see 5:18,20).

In other words, the phrase 'the day of the LORD' refers to an event (which might actually take quite a few days, as did the fall of Jerusalem) when the LORD will step in explosively, decisively and dramatically in judgement, punishing the wicked, overturning the powers, pouring out his wrath upon the nations and rescuing and restoring the faithful.

When Obadiah says, then, that 'the day of the LORD is near upon all the nations', he is not saying that he believes that the whole world is about to end once and for all, but rather that 'God is about to intervene and straighten things out dramatically. When he does so, it will be across the nations. So it will certainly include Edom.'

Of course, before the final 'day of the LORD' at the return of Christ, these international payback interventions of God, these 'days of the LORD' within history leave some evil undealt with and some good unestablished. For this reason, each historical 'day of the LORD' leaves us waiting for the next one, and that may explain why the biblical references to 'the day of the LORD' are almost all future: instead of reflecting on past 'days of the LORD', our attention is drawn to the future. Yes, the fall of the northern kingdom in 722 BC was the day of the LORD; it was 'God steps in to execute justice'. But still more was needed. Then the fall of Jerusalem in 587 BC was also the day of the LORD; it, too, was 'God steps in to execute justice'. But still more was needed. The decisive judgement on the Edomites was the day of the LORD; it was 'God steps in to execute justice' (see how Malachi talks about it in 1:3–5). But still more was needed. And so it goes on. There have been other, even more dramatic, 'days' of the LORD (the cross and resurrection of Jesus, the day of Pentecost and the destruction of Jerusalem in AD 70), yet still, while we remain short of the new heavens and the new earth, we continue to look for the final, last 'day of the LORD' (see 1 Thes. 5:2; Rom. 2:5,16; Phil. 2:16).

UPON ALL THE NATIONS

We noticed in Chapter 2 that the nations are mentioned four times in the book of Obadiah. The first two times the nations are mentioned, they are the agents or spectators of judgement (vv. 1–2), but now they are the objects of judgement. While in the first half of the book, with the people of God devastated, the threatened judgement of Edom was from the nations (v. 1), or direct from God (vv. 3–4) or allies (v. 7), in the second half of the book it is the people of God themselves who are the agents of judgement and who rule over Edom (vv. 18,21).

The fact that God is going to intervene to judge all the nations means that there is no way that Edom can escape (see also Deut. 32:35–36; Joel 3:2; Zech. 14:1,3). The fact that justice will be done to all the nations shows that Obadiah is not an instance of nationalistic chauvinism (the people of Judah being racially or nationally prejudiced against the Edomites), but rather of universal accountability to the global Sovereign.

AS YOU HAVE DONE, IT SHALL BE DONE TO YOU

The 'you' is, of course, still Edom. This principle—sometimes called the *lex talionis* (law of retaliation or retribution)—is basic to the exercise of justice and can be seen again and again in Obadiah. Proud and gloating Edom will be humbled and covered in shame (vv. 2–3,11,10); Edom, which watched the pillage, will itself be pillaged (vv. 11–14,6); Edom, which harassed the survivors, will itself have no survivors (vv. 14,18); Edom, which 'cut off' God's people, will itself be 'cut off' (vv. 14,9–10); Edom, which was treacherous, will itself experience treachery (vv. 10,12,7); Edom, the dispossessor, will itself be dispossessed (vv. 14,7,9); Edom, the thief and plunderer, will itself be robbed and plundered (vv. 13,5–6). Here in 15*b*, the principle is explicitly stated (see also Ezek. 35:15; Prov. 12:14; 19:17; Joel 3:4,7; Matt. 7:2).

YOUR DEEDS [RECOMPENSE/REWARD] SHALL RETURN ON YOUR OWN HEAD

'Deeds' or 'reward' means 'your dealings—the things you have done' and is a further statement that the Edomites are not being punished arbitrarily but are getting what they deserve. (The word is also used in Judg. 9:16; Ps. 28:4; 94:2; Isa. 3:11; 59:18; 66:6; Jer. 51:6; Lam. 3:64.)

FOR AS YOU HAVE DRUNK ... AND SHALL BE AS THOUGH THEY HAD NEVER BEEN
Until this point in the book of Obadiah, the only people directly addressed are the Edomites (see vv. 2–4,5,7,9,10–15). As mentioned above, some readers think that this changes in verse 15 and that the 'you' of verse 16 must mean the Jews. We have seen that this is both unwarranted and unnecessary.

The idea of drinking the cup or wine of God's wrath is an important and biblical idea. (See study questions below). However, in contrast to almost every other biblical use of the image of drinking God's wrath (the one exception is Ps. 60:3), here neither the word 'wrath' nor any particular vessel ('bowl' or 'cup') is mentioned. The idea of verse 16 is not that the Jews will drink God's wrath (as mentioned in the Introduction; the dimension of God punishing the sins of the Jews in the fall of Jerusalem is absent from Obadiah, not because it was not important, but because Obadiah was focusing upon the brother-to-brother relationship and announcing what would happen to the Edomites). Rather, the thought is that, just as the Edomites drank in mad and wicked revelry, so God will make all the nations (Edom included) drink and keep drinking, and get more and more drunk, until they are so utterly soaked that they pass from consciousness and never get up again. (This, too, is an image of wrath or judgement, but it is not the same as drinking God's wrath.)

'My holy mountain' or 'the mountain of my holiness' is a way of referring to Jerusalem and, in particular, Jerusalem as the location of the temple. The Edomites' mad revelry was doubly wicked: not only was it an evil way of reacting to the destruction of Jerusalem, but also it constituted a further desecration of the holy place.

'As though they had never been' does not mean that they will be annihilated (biblical judgement/destruction is not annihilationist). It means that, just as God can make 'somethings' out of nothing, so he can make nothing out of 'somethings'. The nations, with all their pomp, might and self-reliance, will be, on the day when God steps in to set things straight and to execute justice, removed from the stage (see also Isa. 29:7–8; 41:11–12; Zeph. 1:3,18).

Study questions

1. Look up the thirty or so references in the paragraph above about Old Testament usage of the phrase 'the day of the LORD' and list some of the features of these 'put-things-straight' interventions by God. Then carry over these features to the cross and resurrection of the Lord Jesus Christ and to the return of Christ and final judgement, and see how both of these are illuminated by the Old Testament idea of 'the day of the LORD'.

2. Although I have argued that the idea of drinking the cup of God's wrath is not really what is going on in verse 16, nevertheless it is an important study. Some of the key passages to follow up are: Numbers 5; Job 21:19–20; Psalm 23:5; 60:3; 75:8; Isaiah 51:17–23; 63:6; Jeremiah 25:15–29; 48:26–27; 49:12; 51:7–8; 51:39; Lamentations 4:21; Ezekiel 23:31–34; Habakkuk 2:16; Zechariah 12:2; Mark 14:36; Revelation 14:10; 16:19; 19:15. This theme climaxes with the Lord Jesus Christ: in spite of recoiling from the awfulness of coming under the curse of God, he took the cup of God's wrath—the cup that brings a bitter curse—and drank it so that his people, the sinners who deserve to be consumed by God's wrath, wouldn't have to drink it. In turn, remembering his death in their place and rejoicing in the favour of God which is upon them in Jesus, the people of God take up the cup of blessing, the cup of thanksgiving, and rejoice of the participation in the benefits of the death and life of Jesus.

3. Think of other examples in the Bible where 'the punishment fits the crime'. What is the difference between thinking of this as true justice and thinking of it as vengeful retaliation? Why is it actually a *good* thing that wickedness is fully and fittingly punished?

4. List some empires, famous figures, great products, institutions or sports teams that looked at one time as though they would last for ever and now are 'as though they had never been'. Apply Obadiah 16d to some of the most intimidating powers, institutions and people of our time.

5. How does Romans 12:19–21 relate the certainty of future judgement by God to the way in which I should relate to my enemies in the present?

6. Sometimes it is thought that Jesus did away with the *lex talionis* in his statements in Matthew 5:38–48. Discuss the following summary of the relationship between what he says there and what we read in Obadiah 15:

- Every sin must receive its full and fitting punishment.
- No punishment is ever dismissed—it is either borne by the guilty person or it may be voluntarily borne or absorbed by the innocent.
- When Jesus says, 'Do not resist the one who is evil' and so on in Matthew 5:38–39, he is not saying that we can just dismiss the idea of punishment, but rather that, in personal relations (not in matters of crime and punishment in society), his disciples are to 'absorb' the cost or wrong of evil.
- Ultimately, every sin receives its full and fitting punishment either on the cross of Jesus or in hell.

Note

1. See Douglas Stuart's commentary for the beginnings of thoughts along the same lines: **Douglas Stuart,** *Hosea–Jonah* (Word Biblical Commentary; Waco, TX: Word, 1987).

Putting the world to rights (vv. 17–21)

It's been a long climb, and most of the way it's been raining, but you've now reached the top and, as you do so, the clouds clear, the sun comes out and you have a truly fantastic view of the most breathtaking landscape you have ever seen in your life. Not only was the climb more than worth it, you also know that you'll never see the world the same again after today. Obadiah 17–21 is the view from the top of the mountain—Mount Zion, as it happens! These verses describe the world as it should be, the world put back together through the saving intervention of God. This happened with particular historical judgements upon the Edomites. It happened decisively with the completed work of the Lord Jesus Christ. It is happening progressively through the spread of the gospel in the power of the Holy Spirit. And it will happen climactically at the end of history with the return of Jesus and the completion of the new creation which began on Easter Day.

Obadiah, still speaking God's words to the Edomites with the exiled people of God as the real hearers, now turns to the impact upon the people of God of the decisive international setting-things-straight, called the day of the LORD, which he has announced. This entails deliverance, possession and rule for the people of God and climaxes in the establishment and recognition of the fact that the LORD is universal King. Raabe sees something of a pattern in these verses:

destiny of Zion (v. 17)
    repossession of the land (v. 17)
        victory over enemy (v. 18)
    repossession of the land (vv. 19–20)
destiny of Zion (v. 21)[1]

Deliverance and victory (vv. 17–18)

(v. 17a) *But in Mount Zion there shall be those who escape,*

(v. 17b) *and it shall be holy,*

(v. 17c) *and the house of Jacob shall possess their own possessions.*

Questions of how these verses are to be understood in the broader sweep of God's saving rule over human history are addressed in Chapters 9 and 10 below, but Matthew Henry summarizes it like this:

Mount Zion is the gospel-church, from which the New-Testament law *went forth*, Isaiah 2:3. There salvation shall be preached and prayed for; to the gospel-church those are added who *shall be saved*; and for those who come in faith and hope to this Mount Zion deliverance shall be wrought from wrath and the curse, from sin, and death, and hell, while those who continue afar off shall be left to perish ... [T]he gospel-church shall be set up among the heathen, and shall replenish the earth.[2]

This verse is taken up in Joel 2:32 and in the surrounding paragraphs in Joel (see especially 3:17–21), where it is seen more fully what it means for God to reside on Mount Zion and sanctify it.

BUT IN MOUNT ZION THERE SHALL BE THOSE WHO ESCAPE

'Mount Zion', originally the name for the elevation in Jerusalem which, once captured, became the city of David, soon came to apply to the whole area of the temple built by Solomon and then, from this, to the city of Jerusalem or to the people of God, so far as their home was at the temple worshipping the LORD. 'Zion' thus combines a number of ideas, but the most important for its use in this verse are that Mount Zion is God's holy dwelling place where he meets with and protects his people and that it is a mountain representing a kingdom or rule, namely, the rule of the LORD.

As mentioned above at verse 14, the Edomites did their best to ensure that there were no 'survivors' or 'escapees'. They failed because here, in the centre of the storm of judgement, there is escape or deliverance for

God's people. (The ESV rightly translates the singular noun which in the Hebrew is 'escape' or 'deliverance' as a collective noun signifying 'those who escape'. This relates to the idea of a remnant which God delivers and purifies. See Gen. 45:7; Judg. 21:17; 2 Kings 19:30–31; 1 Chr. 4:43; Ezra 9:8,13–15; Isa. 4:2; 10:20; 37:31–32; Jer. 50:28; 51:50; Ezek. 6:8–9; 7:16; 14:22; 24:26–27; Joel 2:32.)

AND IT SHALL BE HOLY

Among other things, it shall be a sanctuary and therefore inviolable (see Joel 3:17).

AND THE HOUSE OF JACOB SHALL POSSESS THEIR OWN POSSESSIONS

The word translated 'possess' here comes to dominate the last few verses of the book. It is a commonly used word in the Old Testament. In family or legal contexts, it usually means 'inherit'. When the object of the verb is people, then it means 'dispossess'. When the object of the verb is territory, it means 'possess'.

In this verse, there is textual uncertainty about the noun 'possessions', which then feeds back into how we understand the 'possess' verb. The noun might be 'dispossessors', in which case the verb will mean 'subdue', 'conquer' or 'dispossess'—as it does when the object is people. Or the noun might be 'possessions', in which case the verb will mean 'possess', 'inherit'—as it does when the object is territory.

If we read the noun as 'possessions', there are still two ways in which the sentence could be understood: with 'possessions' either meaning the promised ancient inheritance (see Exod. 6:8; Ps. 136:21–22; Ezek. 11:15; 33:24) or the things that have been taken from them.

However, with all three of these possibilities, the ultimate outcome is the same: the people of God will take back from the Edomites (and others) what has been taken from them and so will come into full possession of the promised inheritance.

(v. 18*a*) *The house of Jacob shall be a fire,*
(v. 18*b*) *and the house of Joseph a flame,*
(v. 18*c*) *and the house of Esau stubble;*
(v. 18*d*) *they shall burn them and consume them,*
(v. 18*e*) *and there shall be no survivor for the house of Esau,*
(v. 18*f*) *for the* LORD *has spoken.*

The image used here is readily understood. 'The house of Jacob' and 'the house of Joseph' are two ways of describing the people of God. 'The house of Esau' describes the Edomites. God's people will be agents of his wrath and used by him to destroy the Edomites utterly. Key parallels are found in Ezekiel 25:14 and Numbers 24:18.

THE HOUSE OF JACOB ... AND THE HOUSE OF JOSEPH

The northern kingdom (which ended with the destruction of Samaria in 722 BC and the exile to Assyria from which none returned) was sometimes referred to as 'the house of Joseph' (see 1 Kings 11:28; Ps. 77:15; Amos 5:6).

'Jacob' might stand for the southern kingdom or it might stand for the whole people of God from all twelve tribes (as it does in Ps. 22:23). David Baker succinctly addresses this: 'In either case, all of the tribes, those previously exiled by Assyria and those now taken by Babylonia, will be involved in Edom's judgement (cf. also Ezr. 6:17; 8:35, where all twelve tribes of Israel are represented).'[3] That is to say that, already within the Old Testament period, the thought had emerged that the returnees of the southern kingdom either brought with them, or themselves in covenant represented, those of the northern kingdom such that the reoccupation of the land was a reuniting of the divided kingdom.

A FIRE ... A FLAME

The image is plain: God's holy presence is like fire. This is not always wrathful. After all, with his people in the thorn affliction of Egypt, God does not consume the bush; and God's fire on his people on the day of

Pentecost does not consume them but is a Spirit crown which restores their lost glory and empowers them to advance the kingdom. However, when God's holy presence meets wickedness, then it most certainly does come as consuming wrath (see Isa. 10:17; 33:11; 47:14; Exod. 15:7; Ps. 18:8; Lam. 1:13; Amos 1:4). And here in verse 18, it is the judicial destruction of the wicked which is in view, though, given what is coming in verse 21, it is unlikely that Obadiah and his hearers actually envisaged the use of military force and physical violence, killing every Edomite they could find, as the way in which they would come into their possessions.

Certainly the words 'and there shall be no survivor for the house of Esau' are those which come from holy war language passages (such as Num. 21:35; Josh. 8:22; 10:28–43; Deut. 2:34; 3:3). Edom had tried to eliminate Israel but had failed (vv. 14,17). Israel, however, will conquer utterly (see Jer. 42:17; 44:14; Lam. 2:22).

As already noted in verse 9, however, this does not mean the physical destruction of each and every Edomite human being. Malachi 1:3–4 suggests that the judgement on Edom has fallen even though some individual Edomites are alive. Obadiah 21 implies that some Edomites will dwell under the righteous rule of God's people. And the language of 'consuming' does not require total annihilation: 'As Jacob had been devoured [Jer. 10:25; Ps. 14:4; Micah 3:3; Zech. 12:6] so will Edom be consumed.'[4]

The New Testament continues to regard God's people as a people of fire (see Acts 2:3; Rom. 12:11 [boil, be hot in the Spirit]; Rev. 8:5; 11:5). They engage in a war which is not against flesh and blood but against spiritual forces and which is conducted not by military means but by the spiritual weaponry of a righteous life and dependence upon God (Eph. 6:10–18; 2 Cor. 10:3–6). The fire they call down from heaven is not to destroy men in the sense of killing them as men (as happened in 2 Kings 1 and was intended in Luke 9:51–56) but to destroy men 'as wicked'. When the transforming fire of the Spirit falls in this way (as in the return visit to Samaria in Acts 8), the result is not that there are no men standing, but that there are no wicked men standing. The dross of wickedness is consumed, but the gold of humanness is refined. Thus Matthew Henry's and John Trapp's comments on Obadiah 18, far from being a 'spiritualizing' of the prophet's words, actually represent a reading properly informed by the work of Christ and the nature of kingdom warfare since Pentecost. Henry simply says, 'This is fulfilled … [i]n the conversion of multitudes by the grace of Christ; the gospel … Those that are not refined as gold by fire of the gospel shall be consumed as dross by it.'5 And Trapp remarks,

Those of them that were converted by the preaching of the Gospel ceased to be either Edomites or Jews and became Christians. The Apostles burning with the zeal of God's glory and love to men's souls, devoured and wasted the infidelity, idols and vices of the Gentiles wherever they came preaching. Hence Chrysostom saith, Peter was a man made all of fire, walking among stubble.6

Unquestionably, military language is used in the New Testament, but it speaks of the sword of the Spirit (Eph. 6), of 'passions … which wage war against your soul' (1 Peter 2:11), of holy violence against selfishness and sin ('take up your cross', Luke 9:23; 14:27; '… put to death the misdeeds of the body', Rom. 8:13; '… put to death what is earthly in you', Col. 3:5; '… cut it off and throw it away', Matt. 5:30) and of conducting warfare through the worship of God (Rev. 6 and 8).

AND THE HOUSE OF ESAU [FOR] STUBBLE

Stubble is light, insubstantial and eminently combustible (see also Exod. 5:12; 15:7; Ps. 83:13; Isa. 5:24; 40:24; 47:14; Mal. 4:1). In Scripture, humans start as insubstantial as dust and are meant, in Christ, to become heavier and shinier (more glorious) so that as a bejewelled and golden bride they match the gold and ivory bridegroom, the Lord Jesus Christ. They are meant to move from one degree of glory (heaviness and shininess) to another. But when humans rebel against God, they are like chaff which the wind blows away (Ps. 1; Dan. 2); or they 'return to dust' (Eccles. 3); or they are like hay or stubble, fit only to be burned (Matt. 3; 1 Cor. 3; Obad. 18).

FOR THE LORD HAS SPOKEN

This phrase is necessary to remind the hearers that it is the sure word of God and not the speculative or optimistic word of a mere man that has announced that which would otherwise be almost unbelievable, namely, the complete restoration of God's people in verse 17 and the complete destruction of their enemies in verse 18.

Possessing the land (vv. 19–20)

(v. 19a) *Those of the Negeb shall possess Mount Esau,*

(v. 19b) *and those of the Shephelah shall possess the land of the Philistines;*

(v. 19c) *they shall possess the land of Ephraim and the land of Samaria,*

(v. 19d) *and Benjamin shall possess Gilead.*

(v. 20a) *The exiles of this host of the people of Israel*

(v. 20b) *shall possess the land of the Canaanites as far as Zarephath,*

(v. 20c) *and the exiles of Jerusalem who are in Sepharad*

(v. 20d) *shall possess the cities of the Negeb.*

The details of these verses contain many difficulties relating to textual uncertainty, apparently missing verbs and the identification of particular places that are mentioned. The overall thrust of the verses, however, is very clear indeed. Verse 19 refers to people living in the land (whether at the time of the prophecy or looking ahead) and says that, moving south, west, north and east, these people shall possess the territory which God has promised them. Verse 20 refers to people in exile (whether at the time of the prophecy or looking ahead)[7] and says that some shall possess the north (20a–b) and some shall possess the south (20c–d).[8]

Niehaus shows how he thinks verse 19 should be read (which is very largely in line with the ESV) by putting in square brackets words which are absent from the Hebrew but should probably be included to make sense of the verse:9

The Negev	shall possess	Mount Esau
and the Shephelah	[shall possess]	the Philistines
they	shall possess	the range of Ephraim
and [they]	[shall possess]	the range of Samaria
and Benjamin	[shall possess]	Gilead

Once again, Matthew Henry lays out the mainstream interpretation: 'The promise here, no doubt, has a spiritual signification, and had its accomplishment in the setting up of the Christian church, the gospel-Israel, in the world, and shall have its accomplishment more and more in the enlargement of it and the additions made to it, till the mystical body is completed.'10

The possible readings for verse 20 are more complicated still but, as mentioned above, they may be summed up by saying, 'The north and south of the expansive territory promised by God to his people shall be possessed by various groups of exiles from various places.'

The kingdom shall be the Lord's (v. 21)

(v. 21a) *Saviours shall go up to Mount Zion*
(v. 21b) *to rule Mount Esau,*
(v. 21c) *and the kingdom shall be the LORD's.*

There are three lines in this last verse of the book, and one of the key 'figures' of the book features in each of them: Mount Zion, Mount Esau and the LORD. This is the climax of the book. God's people are where they should be—ruling from Zion; the Edomites are where they should be—under the righteous rule of God's people; and the LORD is what he should be—the undisputed, fully acknowledged King.

Chapter 8

Given that the defeat of Edom is associated with judgement upon all the nations, this implies the overthrow of all the powers of evil. Mason puts it like this:

What is envisaged is not, in the end, primarily national superiority for Israel, but the universal rule of God as king, removing from his domain all the evil which opposes him and thwarts his purpose. He will eradicate all that which 'Edom' and 'the nations' could be seen to represent and of which they were symbols.[11]

And Barton's comment is equally helpful:

Obadiah is a kind of response to the message of Lamentations, with its fear that YHWH had abandoned his people. It reaffirms that it is truly YHWH who is in charge of what occurs on earth, and who will, in the long run, take steps to reestablish his sovereignty. God is not to be evaded, but his intention is ultimately to establish a new world order characterized by peace, though also by the predominance of his chosen people, Israel.[12]

SAVIOURS SHALL GO UP TO [COME UP ON] MOUNT ZION

'Saviours' relates to the word from which we get the names Joshua and Jesus. Some texts have 'the saved' rather than 'saviours', but that is unjustified. 'Saviours' are those who save, who make salvation happen, who bring about deliverance. (Some other Old Testament uses of the basic word include Deut. 28:29,31; Judg. 3:9,15; 2 Sam. 22:3; 2 Kings 13:5; Neh. 9:27; Ps. 106:21; Isa. 19:20; 43:3,11; 63:8; Hosea 13:4.) Particularly relevant is the use of this word in Nehemiah 9:27 to describe the heroes of the times of the judges. Obadiah does not mention a restored monarchy (not because he does not believe in it) but speaks rather of Spirit-empowered leaders who bring Israel back into liberty and possession of the land after they have been oppressed as a result of their own unfaithfulness.

But 21*a–b* is to be regarded as the climax and the purpose of the repossession activity. The headquarters of the kingdom, the capital city of the people of God, will be back in their hands, and from there they will rule over those who previously have been their worst enemies. Zion was the place of deliverance in verse 17, and the delivered, who are themselves saviours, will now occupy Zion as the place from which, in the power of the LORD, they will rule. The elevation of Mount Zion at the centre of a renewed and righteous world is similar to the thought of Isaiah 2:1–5, and there are also significant parallels with the hope of Zechariah 14.

TO RULE [JUDGE] MOUNT ESAU

Conquering Zion leads to ruling Edom. In the battle of the mountains, Zion will win. But this rule will not be a vindictive taking of vengeance. Rather it will be the rule of righteous judgement, proper law-giving and godly administration. (The word 'judge' carries these ideas in various places: see Gen. 16:5; 31:53; Num. 25:5; Judg. 2:16–19; 3:10; 2 Kings 15:5; 2 Chr. 1:10; Ps. 9:8; 58:11; 96:13; Prov. 29:14; Isa. 33:22; 51:5; Joel 3:2; 3:12.) Renkema puts it well: 'This change of power, however, does not end up in a frenzy of revenge for the evil suffered. The new masters who will lead the people in Zion will also govern Edom with justice as representatives of YHWH's kingship.'[13]

In a way, verse 21 even holds out hope for Edom. Its defeat will result in coming under the righteous rule of the LORD exercised by his people.

AND THE KINGDOM [KINGSHIP] SHALL BE THE LORD'S

The 'kingdom' or the 'kingship' is the royal authority, the undisputed identity and rule as king (see also 1 Sam. 10:16,25; 14:47; 1 Kings 1:46; Ps. 22:28).

This is the summary of the state of affairs that will be brought about by the intervention of God which will bring punishment to Edom, judgement to the nations and restoration to God's people. And in this sense, every time we pray, 'Our Father in heaven, hallowed be your name. Your kingdom come, your will be done, on earth as it is in heaven,' we are praying the book of Obadiah. The world put to rights, the world set straight; God's people delivered from their enemies, used by God to accomplish his righteous purposes, dwelling in his immediate presence, inheriting their promised possessions; and all through the exercise of and leading to the recognition of God's sovereign, saving, splendid kingship: that is how things should be.

Study questions

1. Clearly there are differences among Christians as to how to interpret some of these verses. However, some things are agreed upon by all Christians: if the people of God, at any time, are to enjoy deliverance, possession and rule, then it will be in Christ through our relationship with him. In what ways does Christ now possess (own and have authority over and use of) every piece of territory on the planet? (See Matt. 28:17–20; John 13:1–3; Rom. 4:13; 1 Cor. 3:21–23; Col. 1:15–20; Heb. 1:2; Ps. 2:7–8; 1 Cor. 15:25–28.) And what implications does this have for our attitude to 'real estate'?

2. Explore the idea of warfare and conquest using some of the references given in the comments above. Does this affect the way we read the prophets and sing the psalms?

3. Trace the images of glory as 'weight' and 'shininess' and of sinners as 'lightweight' and 'earthy' through Scripture.

4. Discuss the importance of hope in waging warfare and apply that both to your own battle with sin and to the way in which the persecuted church should use Obadiah 17–21.

5. Describe the way in which Christ rules all things and the ways in which believers do and do not share that rule now.

6. What do we really mean when we pray, 'Your kingdom come'?

7. Meditate upon the picture of the people of God as a 'flame' or 'fire' and draw implications from that for the way we should think about ourselves, our relationship with God and our conduct.

Notes

1 **Paul Raabe,** *Obadiah* (Anchor Bible 24D; New York: Doubleday, 1997), p. 253.

2 **Matthew Henry,** *A Commentary upon the Whole Bible,* vol. iv (1712; [n.d.], Iowa Falls, IA: World Bible Publishers), p. 1276. Comment on vv. 17–21.

3 **David W. Baker, T. Desmond Alexander** and **Bruce K. Waltke,** *Obadiah, Jonah and Micah* (TOTC; Leicester: IVP, 1998), p. 40.

4 Ibid. Comment on v. 18.

5 **Henry,** *Commentary,* p. 1276. Comment on vv. 17–21.

6 **John Trapp,** *A Commentary or Exposition upon the XII Minor Prophets* (London, 1654). Comment on v. 18.

7 The word translated 'exiles' or 'the captivity' is, according to Baker, 'often associated with Judaean deportees after 587 BC (2 Kg 25:27, Ezk 1:2).' **David W. Baker, in David W. Baker, T. Desmond Alexander** and **Bruce K. Waltke,** *Obadiah, Jonah and Micah* (TOTC; Leicester: IVP, 1998). Comment on v. 20. See also Isa. 20:4; 45:13; Jer. 28:4; Amos 1:6.

8 For more detailed investigation of these verses, see **Barton, Raabe** or **Stuart,** details of whose books can be found in the *Further resources* section.

9 **Jeffrey Niehaus,** 'Obadiah', in **Thomas E. McComiskey** (ed.), *The Minor Prophets,* vol. ii (Grand Rapids, MI: Baker, 1993). Comment on v. 19.

10 **Henry,** *Commentary,* p. 1277. Comment on vv. 17–21.

11 **R. Mason,** *Micah, Nahum, Obadiah* (Old Testament Guides; Sheffield: JSOT Press, 1991), p. 102.

12 **John Barton,** *Joel and Obadiah* (OTL; Louisville, KY: Westminster John Knox Press, 2001), p. 158.

13 **Johan Renkema,** *Obadiah* (Historical Commentary on the Old Testament; Leuven: Peeters, 2003), p. 108.

Jesus in Obadiah (3): Obadiah and the gospel (vv. 17–21)

W e often find that light is cast upon how Old Testament prophets are to be understood by the way in which they are used in the New Testament. This certainly applies to Obadiah—in spite of the fact that Obadiah is not quoted in the New Testament at all! The way in which Joel uses Obadiah, combined with the way in which Peter uses Joel on the day of Pentecost, means that Peter's Pentecost sermon helps us understand Obadiah. Similarly, the way in which Obadiah uses Amos, combined with the way in which James uses Amos at the Council of Jerusalem in Acts 15, means that Acts 15 also helps us understand Obadiah. In both cases, we can see clearly that the fulfilment of Obadiah's prophecy is something that happens in the international spread of the gospel of our Lord Jesus Christ.

Obadiah and Joel

Obadiah looks forward to a mighty intervention of God in which God's people shall be delivered. As verse 17 says, 'But in Mount Zion there shall be those who escape.' We do not know exactly when Joel prophesied, but it does seem that, in chapter 2 of the book named after him, he quotes Obadiah 17. The whole section in Joel 2 runs like this:

And it shall come to pass afterwards,
that I will pour out my Spirit on all flesh;
your sons and your daughters shall prophesy,
your old men shall dream dreams,
and your young men shall see visions.

Even on the male and female servants
in those days I will pour out my Spirit.

And I will show wonders in the heavens and on the earth, blood and fire and columns of smoke. The sun shall be turned to darkness, and the moon to blood, before the great and awesome day of the LORD comes. And it shall come to pass that everyone who calls on the name of the LORD shall be saved. For in Mount Zion and in Jerusalem there shall be those who escape, as the LORD has said, and among the survivors shall be those whom the LORD calls.

(Joel 2:28–32)

It is in the second half of verse 32 that Joel is quoting Obadiah—the words 'in Jerusalem there shall be … escape' are exactly the same as they are in Obadiah. They are also linked with the phrase 'as the LORD has said'.[1]

So Joel quotes Obadiah 17 and associates the deliverance it promises with God's coming intervention at the time when there will be a changeover of the worlds. God's Spirit will be poured out, upheavals will take place, one world will end and another will begin. At that time, all who call on the name of the LORD will be saved—and on Mount Zion and in Jerusalem there will be deliverance.

This is a help to us in seeing how we should understand Obadiah because, although Obadiah is not quoted in the New Testament, Joel most certainly is. It is this very section of Joel which Peter uses on the day of Pentecost to explain the apostles' speaking in other languages. Peter replies to the charge that he and the other apostles are drunk by saying that what Joel prophesied is coming about; he then quotes the above Joel 2 passage. Peter is saying that, with the death and resurrection of Jesus, the changeover of the worlds is taking place. An old world is ending—it is in its last days, so it is no wonder that the authorities of that world are shaken and the ordinary folk experiencing upheaval. Its sun is dying and its moon is bleeding because this is the longed-for saving intervention of God to establish a new world. That new world is established with the exaltation and enthronement of Jesus and marked by the outpouring of the Spirit. And at this time of crisis and salvation, deliverance and safety are found by those who call upon the name of the Lord. He goes on to make clear who the Lord is: 'God has made him both Lord and Christ, this Jesus whom you crucified,' and he also explains how people are to call upon his name—by repenting and being baptized in his name (Acts 2:36; 22:16).[2]

All of this suggests that the deliverance mentioned in Obadiah 17, as quoted in a section of Joel which Peter, in turn, quotes on the day of Pentecost, is the deliverance which comes to human beings as they call on the name of the Lord Jesus Christ. No, Obadiah is not quoted by name in the New Testament. But Joel's use of Obadiah and Peter's use of Joel amount to the same thing. The clear conclusion is that the deliverance which Obadiah prophesied is to be had now, in the age of the Spirit, when people from all nations respond to the gospel by calling on the name of the Lord Jesus Christ.

Obadiah and Amos

A similar two-stage journey shows us more of what the New Testament has to say about the fulfilment of another aspect of Obadiah's prophecy: the conquest and possession of verses 18–20.

Amos (9:11–12) says that the time is coming when God will restore his people and they will 'possess the remnant of Edom'. Obadiah, who prophesied two centuries later, takes up and fills out this theme, speaking of how God's people will subdue Edom and 'possess' and judge Mount Esau. One scholar puts it like this:

It is more or less assumed that Obadiah was placed after Amos in the Masoretic canon on the basis of the prophecy of salvation in Am 9:12 in which it is predicted that the remnant of Edom and the nations will be taken once again into the possession of the restored Davidic kingdom. The beginning of the fulfillment of this prophecy is outlined in Obadiah.[3]

Then, at the Council of Jerusalem in Acts 15, we read about discussions in the early church as to how Gentile believers are to be treated. Peter argues from God's work in Cornelius and Paul and Barnabas from God's work in the Gentiles through them. Then James addresses the assembly:

And all the assembly fell silent, and they listened to Barnabas and Paul as they related what signs and wonders God had done through them among the Gentiles. After they finished speaking, James replied, 'Brothers, listen to me. Simeon has related how God first visited the Gentiles, to take from them a people for his name. And with this the words of the prophets agree, just as it is written,

'"After this I will return,
and I will rebuild the tent of David that has fallen;
I will rebuild its ruins,
and I will restore it,
that the remnant of mankind may seek the Lord,
and all the Gentiles who are called by my name,
says the Lord, who makes these things known from of old."

Therefore my judgement is that we should not trouble those of the Gentiles who turn to God, but should write to them to abstain from the things polluted by idols, and from sexual immorality, and from what has been strangled, and from blood. For from ancient generations Moses has had in every city those who proclaim him, for he is read every Sabbath in the synagogues.'

(vv. 12–21)

In brief, James is arguing that, because of the work of Christ, Amos's prophecy is being fulfilled in the spread of the gospel among the Gentiles. The takeover of the world by the true Israel is proceeding apace as the Lord Jesus Christ disciples the nations by the gospel preached in the power of the Spirit.

There are some difficulties in interpreting Acts 15 and relating it to Amos 9.4 Nevertheless, if we were to put a copy of Acts 15 in front of Amos, it is hard to believe that we would hear anything other than laughter and songs from the old prophet. Perhaps he would address James: 'I say "Edom", you say "Adam" ["mankind" in Acts 15:17]; I say "possess", you say "seek the Lord"; but let's not call anything off. This is wonderful! I had never thought that the fulfilment of the prophecy the Lord gave me could look so intensive and so extensive, so deep and so high, so global and so transforming. I never thought that what I said about the fallen "booth of David" could look as good as this—that it pointed to thousands and thousands of Gentiles united with the Davidic king to form a human Zion full of song and indwelt by the Spirit. This is amazing—all glory be to God!'

If we then brought Obadiah to the conversation, he would not be able to contain himself: 'Lord, you're wonderful in all you do. Here was I thinking that, if Nabonidus could give the Edomites a hard time in the mid-sixth century BC, or the Nabataeans could displace them in the fourth century BC, or if John Hyrcanus could force them to be circumcised in the second century BC, then perhaps that would count as success and fulfilment. But now I see what burning up Edomite stubble and taking over Mount Edom really looks like. This is a riot—you mean that all the nations are being taken over by Jesus through the gospel preached in the power of the Spirit? Marvellous and excellent and altogether great! We prophets have been straining to look into these things for centuries [1 Peter 1:10], and now we realize what a "great salvation" is the one which you have brought about through the work of the Lord Jesus Christ.'

In summary, when we look for New Testament help in understanding Obadiah, we find that it comes to us indirectly—through James's use of a part of Amos which Obadiah filled out and built upon. No, Obadiah is not quoted by name in the New Testament. But Obadiah's use of Amos and James's use of Amos amount to the same thing.

The clear conclusion is that the conquest and possession which Obadiah prophesied is to be had now, in the age of the Spirit, when people from all nations respond to the gospel by calling on the name of the Lord Jesus Christ. Obadiah is fulfilled with the takeover of the world which the Gentile mission represents by the Lord Jesus Christ, the True Israel, as the gospel is announced across the nations in the power of the Holy Spirit.

Put Joel, Amos and Acts together and I think you end up saying something like this:

The decisive intervention of God which Obadiah predicted—an intervention in judgement and salvation—is confirmed through the book of Acts to have taken place in the establishment of the new world order, the kingdom of God, the gospel age, the era of the Spirit—all through the completed work of the Lord Jesus Christ. The deliverance which Obadiah prophesied is the salvation and renewal which is found by men, women and children from every nation believing the gospel of the Lord Jesus Christ. The takeover of the world by Israel which Obadiah predicted is the spread of the kingdom through the Gentile mission, as the Lord Jesus, who has all authority in heaven and on earth, disciples the nations and saves the world. He is enthroned at the right hand of God and has been promised all nations as his inheritance and the ends of the earth as his possession; and he is subduing all things to himself through the Spirit-empowered announcement of the gospel. He is waiting to see all his enemies thus subdued and, when this has happened, he will return in glory to usher in the new heavens and the new earth.

Obadiah—rightly understood through Joel, Amos and Acts—is about gospel deliverance and gospel takeover. It is about the advance of the kingdom of God, the building of the church and the progress of world mission.

When does that happen? Right now. Ever since the day of Pentecost. It is true that the straggling, defeated, humiliated exile moment at which Obadiah was delivered was once historically enacted in the life of Christ—when he was on the cross (see Chapter 6 above). But we must not get stuck there: the resurrection and enthronement of King Jesus mean that we are emphatically in the period of verses 17–21. True, it is being realized only progressively, but progressive realization is not postponement, nor watering down or spiritualizing away.

Where is this happening? Not just in greater Palestine but all over the world. Right now, today, as the gospel is preached, Obadiah 17–21 is being fulfilled. Israel's hope has expanded. The world belongs to Israel. The Abrahamic covenant is being fulfilled through the gospel, and that means every family of the earth being blessed through his seed. The glory of a prince lies in the multitude of his subjects and, since our Lord Jesus is the most glorious prince of all, his is the outstanding, the everlasting, the truly international kingdom.

What does this look like? Praise God, you can see it there in Obadiah: rescued and renewed human beings, righteous rule, brotherly love and humility, Spirit-empowered leadership—and all amounting to the thing that, in our right minds, is what we want above all else, 'the kingship shall be the LORD's'. See Chapter 10 for more about this.

Study questions

1. Look at the New Testament passages below which take up Old Testament prophecies and relate them to the completed work of Christ and the spread of the gospel. Compare them with the way in which Joel, Amos and Obadiah have been considered in this chapter.

- Hosea 11:1 in Matthew 2:15
- Zechariah 9:9 in Matthew 21:5
- Isaiah 6:9–10 in Acts 28:26–28
- Deuteronomy 30:13–14 in Romans 10:6–10
- Hosea 13:14 in 1 Corinthians 15:55
- Zechariah 8:16 in Ephesians 4:25
- Jeremiah 31:31–34 in Hebrews 8:8–12
- Exodus 19:6 in 1 Peter 2:9
- Hosea 1:6,9–10 in 1 Peter 2:10

2. When we read the Old Testament after having come to understand that all God's promises are 'Yes' in Jesus Christ, it is like reading a novel the second time around. You begin to notice all sorts of things about events, characters and speeches in earlier parts of the book in the light of what is then revealed in later parts of the book. Consider this in relation to the way in which the following different parts of the Old Testament point to Jesus and the gospel age:

- the sacrificial system set up under Moses
- the history of the judges and the kings
- great hero figures of the Old Testament
- the righteous and wise life described in Proverbs
- the hopes and fears of the psalmists

Notes

1. See **Raabe,** p. 33; or **Bewer, Baker** and **Keil/Delitzsch** on Obadiah v. 17. Details of these books are to be found in the *Further Resources* section.
2. A possible objection is that, at Pentecost, Peter ends his quotation of Joel just before the Obadiah section. I have attempted a lighthearted response to this objection in Appendix 2.
3. **Johan Renkema,** *Obadiah* (Historical Commentary on the Old Testament; Leuven: Peeters, 2003), p. 25.
4. See commentaries on Amos and Acts for more technical discussion of these difficulties.

Jesus in Obadiah (4): Obadiah's dream (vv. 17–21)

Nowadays one should doubt the power of dreams to move our emotions and to change our lives. One of the most powerful speeches in all twentieth-century public life can be summarized and evoked by just four words: 'I have a dream.'[1] The last few verses of Obadiah amount to his dream or vision of how the world should be, and in this chapter we take time to describe the Christ-centred, gospel age ways in which that dream becomes a reality.

We have seen how, in verses 15–16, the decisive intervention of God as Saviour and Judge to defeat the powers, punish wickedness and set things straight has been described. At the end of the book of Obadiah, in verse 21, the state of affairs when God's identity as King is fully acknowledged and experienced is set out. As we saw in Chapter 8, between those two sections, Obadiah gives us seven characteristics of the world as he sees it should and will be:

It is a *Zion world* in which there is *deliverance, holiness* and *possession*, in which *evil is defeated and eliminated*, and in which *saviours* exercise *righteous rule*.

Once we have read the New Testament, we know that such a world is the very world established and being expanded in Christ by the Spirit, through the gospel, in the church, across the nations, down the generations and to be consummated in the new heavens and the new earth.

So we ask Obadiah, 'Obadiah, what have you seen? Do you have a dream? Have you been to the mountain top? What is your vision? How should the world be, Obadiah, and how will it be? What will things look like when God intervenes in the way that you have prophesied he will?'

And Obadiah replies by describing a world characterized by the seven features we mentioned above. He tells us about:

A Zion world (vv. 17,21)

Here we see that Zion is the heart of Obadiah's dream for the future. Zion is where God acts to defeat evil and restore his people (v. 17), and Zion is the centre of the newly established world of righteous rule (v. 21). That is to say that the world has a centre and that that centre is where it should be—where God dwells. God is Deliverer, Sanctifier and King, and thus the place where he dwells is a place of salvation, sanctity and security. It is a place where people are set free, made holy and live in peace. And it is right that such a place should be the capital city of the world, the headquarters of the kingdom of God.

Deliverance, escape and survival (v. 17)

Using the word which is also used in verse 14 for 'survivors', Obadiah shows that the opposite of what the Edomites intended will take place. The Edomites intended that there should be no survival or deliverance, but escape, survival and deliverance are exactly what there will be. Those who were oppressed will be vindicated; those who were crushed are breathing again. The monster has been defeated, the threat has been lifted, and those who were in distress have come out of the darkness into light, out of the storm into the calm—they are safe and secure on the shore.

Holiness (v. 17)

What was defiled by the Babylonian pigs and the demonic Edomites will be made clean. What was profane will be made holy, set apart and put to God's use. All things will be taken from one degree of glory to another. That which was earth will be made bronze, that which was bronze will be made silver, and that which was silver will be made gold. Everything will be sanctified, beautified and glorified. The whole world will be under the city, and the whole city will be set apart, a sanctuary for God.

Possession and inheritance (vv. 18–20)

The possession of the land which was promised in Genesis 15, commanded in Deuteronomy 1 and prophesied in Amos 9 will become a reality. The people will enter into the promise. For long ages, they have gazed at the lands around, wondering when they will possess them as God said they will. They have wondered, 'This area, or that territory, or this part of the land—how long will they remain in enemy hands as pagan countries?' The answer comes: now is the time when the LORD's empire will expand and extend so that everywhere his people set their feet comes under their possession and becomes a place in which they can settle in security and live in peace.

Judgement fire (v. 18)

God himself is a consuming fire: he devours by fire the sacrifices that are put onto the altar; he descends in fire to consume the sacrifice on Carmel; and, when wickedness comes into contact with him, it is defeated and eradicated. So now his people are to be a fiery people. They will call down fire from heaven, they will breathe fire from their mouths and they will have fire upon their heads. Bringing the holy judgement of God, they will devour and consume the wicked.

Deliverers or saviours (v. 21)

The picture here might be of elite troops who come up to take the last remaining stronghold. But, given the way that exactly the same word is used in Nehemiah 9:27 to describe the heroes of the book of Judges, and given that the usual Jewish hope for a restoration of a Davidic king is not explicit in Obadiah, it is likely that we are to think of Spirit-empowered leaders like the judges. There will be Ehuds—but right-handed; Gideons—but not idolatrous; Jephthahs—but not wilful; and Samsons—but not adulterous.

Righteous rule (v. 21)

In the Zion-centred world of which Obadiah prophesies there will be just laws, true government and right decisions. The world will be as it should be. The elder (Esau) will serve the younger (Jacob), but this will not be a repeat of the Edomites' sin which caused the whole prophecy to be given. It is not that, because the Edomites were malicious to the Jews, when the new world arrives, the Jews will be malicious to the Edomites; rather, though the Edomites were false brothers to the Jews, when Mount Zion rules over Mount Esau, the Jews will be true brothers to the Edomites and will rule in brotherly love, order and justice. Reversal and transformation, rather than a repeat of the old bad ways, mark the arrival of the new world.

Thus Obadiah has his dream. He has been to the mountain top, and this is the world that he has seen: the Zion world of deliverance, holiness, possession, judgement, saviours and righteous rule.

He sees the rescued and vindicated people of God live in the set-apart, holy mountain capital city where God dwells; he sees them used as agents of the eradication of wickedness and the defeat of evil; he sees them as the restored Israel, as full possessors of the promised inheritance; and he sees them acting as the Spirit-empowered instruments of God's righteous rule.

And all this means, demonstrates and results from the kingship of the LORD. The LORD is King, and the fact is now acknowledged and experienced.

This is all very well—it is a comprehensible and coherent set of things for a Jewish prophet to hope for in the sixth century BC—but what now?

Well, imagine for a few moments placing the prophet Obadiah in front of a large screen and then playing to him the film of all history. You watch his reactions in order to gauge what he thinks is happening at any given moment.

Obadiah watches the work of Nebuchadnezzar in 583 BC and of Nabonidus in 553 BC, when these emperors gave the Edomites a hard time and, just for a moment, he wonders whether this is the beginning of the fulfilment of his prophecy. Then he realizes that there is no way that these events can be compared with the world which God revealed to him in his vision.

He keeps watching and sees the Nabataeans displacing the Edomites in the fourth century before Christ, and he hears Malachi declare from God the fact that, at one level, this is the decisive defeat of the Edomites which he, Obadiah, had prophesied. But the defeat of the Edomites was not even half the story, let alone the whole thing. Obadiah continues to watch, unimpressed by the forced circumcision of the Edomites in the second century before Christ. There has *got* to be more, surely.

And then, as Obadiah watches, *he* comes. The Lord Jesus Christ arrives and lives, dies and rises to rule over all things. Now what does Obadiah see?

He sees one who *is* Zion—who is the embodiment of God's presence as Deliverer, Sanctifier and King.

He sees one who is the focus of God's greatest ever deliverance—the resurrection-enthronement of the crucified.

He sees one who is holy as no other is holy—set apart as the Son of God in power and installed on God's holy hill of Zion to rule all things.

He sees one who is given universal possession, the nations as his inheritance and the ends of the earth as his possession. He sees him taking possession of the entire world.

He sees the fiery presence of the wickedness-destroying, serpent-crushing, evil-eradicating holy one of God.

He sees one who is Deliverer or Saviour above all others—the Spirit-empowered hero warrior who takes over strongholds as if there's no tomorrow.

And he sees one who exercises God's righteous rule over all the earth.

And Obadiah shouts and screams with delight. He does not say, 'That can't be what my prophecy meant because I couldn't imagine that at the time I uttered it.' He does not complain that grammatical-historical exegesis can't arrive at Jesus from Obadiah 15–21. He laughs and dances and exults that God's intervention is of this unimaginable glory.

We almost have to hold Obadiah down. We tell him that, though he is absolutely right that Jesus *is* the arrival of the new dreamt-of world, the fulfilment of his vision, there is actually more to see. Watch this, we say—and then we show him the spread of the gospel over the world, the building of the church and the advance of the kingdom down the centuries and the millennia. And as he watches, he comes to realize that the Lord Jesus Christ is what is sometimes called a 'corporate Messiah', that is, he is not an isolated individual but is head of a family, a body, a whole race, and that the things which are true of Christ are true of all the members of this family too, by virtue of their union with him.

And looking at them—the millions and millions of men and women and children united to Jesus as, through the gospel, the Holy Spirit gives them saving faith in him—Obadiah sees the same realities being played out.

He sees that these people themselves 'come to Zion' (Heb. 12). The capital city of the world, the headquarters of the kingdom, now in the throne room of heaven, is their home. They are citizens of Zion and, in Jesus, they live where God lives.

He sees that they are a delivered people and that the great deliverance of the resurrection is theirs too. Because they are joined to Jesus, the verdict, 'I'm perfectly satisfied with you', which God pronounced over Jesus in the resurrection, is pronounced over them, too. Jesus was handed over for their trespasses and raised for their justification.

He sees that these are a set-apart people. The work of Jesus has moved them from profane to holy, from unclean to clean, and is changing them from one degree of glory to another. They are being beautified and glorified and are now and for ever set apart for God's special use.

He sees that they are possessors of the world. In Christ, they are blessed with every spiritual blessing in the heavenly realms. They have come to completeness in him. All things are theirs in him—life and death and heaven and hell and the present and the future: everything. They are co-heirs with Christ of life, the universe and glory.

He sees that they are a fiery people. Fire rests on their heads (Acts 2), comes out of their mouths (Rev. 11:5), burns in their hearts (Rom. 12:11—'boil, be hot in the Spirit'), and is called down by them from heaven (Rev. 8). Remember Chrysostom's comment that 'Peter was a man made all of fire, walking among stubble'.[2] And the fire is burning up evil in all sorts of ways and directions. Evil in their own lives is burned up by the purging process of 'sanctification'. Evil is burned up as they call down and enact God's judgement on the wicked. Evil is burned up as they announce the gospel in the power of the Spirit and as men, women and children are consumed and transformed by that good news.

He sees a Spirit-empowered people who act energetically as warrior-heroes, pulling down strongholds in the name of Jesus and occupying them for his glory. Ehuds and Deborahs and Gideons and Jephthahs and Samsons—the mighty ones of the kingdom of Jesus who themselves bring release and safety to others.

And he sees righteous rule being exercised as those joined to Jesus begin to exercise his dominion in their spheres of influence—their tongues, minds, children, churches, neighbourhoods, workplaces and nations.

Now Obadiah cannot contain himself. He was right to think that the new world he had dreamed of came and was embodied in Jesus. But now that he sees that it consists of and is inhabited by millions and millions and millions of men, women and children from every corner of the earth over generation after generation, he can hardly believe it.

But still we keep him in his seat. 'It's not over yet,' we say. And we take him to the end of history and to the return of Christ in glory. We show him the new heavens and the new earth, where God is dwelling with humans and the whole earth is Zion. We show him the ultimate rescue, escape and deliverance. We show him a holiness he thought he could never dream, and a possessed inheritance which reaches to the limits of the cosmos and to a share in the glory of God himself. We show him the utter eradication of evil and its exclusion from the world. We show him a people who dwell in the fire of God and are not consumed, a people exercising strength, valour and righteous rule beyond his wildest imagination. And we say—and remember, this is not some extra thing, some addition—'This is the outworking, the consequence, the logic of your right answer—that the Lord Jesus Christ himself was and embodied and established the new world, the dream world of your vision.'

This, then, is Obadiah's dream made reality. The vision of Obadiah has come in the person of Jesus. The world as it should be is a Christ-defined, Christ-shaped and Christ-centred world. It is the world of the spreading gospel and the growing church.

It is the world which is subverting and replacing the old doomed world of rebellion against God.

It is the world which is the destiny, hope and calling of space and time, and the human race and the universe.

It is what is summed up in Obadiah 21c—'The kingdom shall be the LORD's.'

It is what we pray for daily in the Lord's prayer—'Hallowed be your name. Your kingdom come, your will be done, on earth as it is in heaven.'

It is what we mean when we say that 'for me to live is Christ'.

It is our goal and priority as we seek first the kingdom of God and his righteousness.

This and this alone—this Christ-defined, Christ-shaped and Christ-centred world—is what our lives are meant to be about. If they are not, we are wasting them. If they are, Obadiah's vision is becoming a reality—to the praise and glory of God.

Study questions

1. Compare the sevenfold description of the world put back together again in Obadiah 17–21 with the characteristics of the kingdom of God as described in the New Testament and with the characteristics of the new heavens and the new earth, also as described in the New Testament.

2. Run through each of the seven features and outline how they affect:

a) our attitude to the Lord Jesus Christ as the one who secures and embodies these things;

b) our self-understanding as those who, in union with Christ, are growing into and are destined to enjoy these things.

Notes

1. Martin Luther King's speech on 28 August 1963.

2. See the quotation from John Trapp in Chapter 8.

1. In one verse, for children.
2. In three verses, for children.
3. In four verses, for all.

1. Obadiah

'Pride and hate' is a wobbly tower
which God brings crashing down.
But life in Jesus' powerful hand
brings rescue, land and crown.

2. Obadiah

The prophet Obadiah tells
the Edomites their fate:
'God's judgement falls upon you all
who live in pride and hate.'

He also tells God's broken few
(just now a tiny band):
'You shall be rescued and shall rule
as owners of the land.'

These promises we see God keeps
in Jesus Christ our King.
The world is his, we reign in him:
to him all praise we bring.

3. Obadiah

Suggested tunes (CMD, iambic):
Ellacombe, Massachusetts

'Perched in your craggy fortresses
set high above the ground,
you think you are untouchable,
but I will bring you down.
Your height won't save, your wealth
won't save,
your friends will traitors prove;

your wisdom and your mighty men—
they cannot rescue you.

'Where I demanded brother's love,
you watched with vicious hate;
malicious, cruel and arrogant,
you mocked my people's fate.
My wrath will crush you, Edomites,
you vile, hubristic crew.
I'll cut you down and cut you off
so none remembers you.

'When I step into history
(that Day is near at hand),
you'll drink in pain, not revelry
and lose the power to stand.
But on Mount Zion I will save
and vindicate my own;
from there they'll take and rule the land
and there I'll set my throne.'

Now what God by his prophet said
he has through Jesus done.
Deliverance, possession, rule—
achieved by God's great Son.
Discipling nations, conquering powers,
he's ruling all things now.
And as it's seen that he is King,
before him all shall bow.

Who is being addressed in Obadiah 16*a*?

It may be that the correct translation of verse 1*b* is 'concerning Edom' rather than 'to Edom', but even if it is, Edom is directly addressed over and over again through the prophecy—in verses 2, 3, 4, 5, 7, 9, 10–14 and 15 (various commentators rightly explaining that this functions as an 'apostrophe'). The reader expects, therefore, that verse 16 is also addressed to Edom: 'For as you have drunk on my holy mountain, so all the nations shall drink continually ...'

However, a large number of interpreters think otherwise. They think that the 'you' of verse 16 indicates a change of addressee and should be identified with the people of Judah. There are three main ways, then, of understanding verse 16, namely:

1. As you Edomites have drunk God's wrath, so the nations will, too ...

2. As you Edomites have drunk in joy at Judah's fall, so the nations will drink the cup of wrath ...

3. As you Judahites have drunk the cup of wrath, so the nations will drink the cup of wrath ...

I will give no attention to option 1, because it seems to me that it is ruled out by the temporal orientation of the entire prophecy, namely, that Edom has yet to be punished. As to options 2 and 3, there are arguments in both directions:

A. The people of Judah

1. The grammatical form of the 'you' is different from that used previously in Obadiah. Up until this point, all the direct addresses to the

Edomites have used the singular form, but here in verse 16 the 'you' is in plural form: 'You [singular] have been doing this and you [singular] have been doing that and I will do this to you [singular]. And as you [plural] have drunk …' The argument runs that a change in the grammatical form must indicate that someone different is being addressed.

2. The focus of the prophecy now shifts from a particular judgement upon the Edomites to a more general judgement upon the nations and to the restoration of the people of Judah. This would be an appropriate moment to turn from addressing Edom directly to addressing the people of Judah directly.

3. If it is the Edomites who are addressed, then it probably requires that the drinking in the two parts of the verse are different sorts of drinking. This would be odd.

4. Whichever people are the 'you' of verse 16*a*, they have drunk 'on my holy mountain'. Surely that is more likely to be the people of Judah than the Edomites.

5. The picture of the 'cup of wrath' being drunk first by God's people and then handed over to the nations is one which is found explicitly elsewhere in Scripture, in Isaiah 51:17–23.

B. The Edomites

1. It would be surprising if a major change of addressee were not more definitely signalled than by a small change of grammatical form. This is especially the case given that there is already a bit of toing and froing between the grammatical forms of those addressed or referred to in Obadiah (for example, Edom is feminine in v. 1 and masculine in v. 2; the people of Judah are both singular and plural in v. 13) as well as in other minor prophets.

2. The focus of the prophecy does not shift so dramatically at this point as might at first be thought. Although 'all the nations' are mentioned in both verses 15 and 16, this is in order to underline the inescapability of the

LORD's judgement of Edom. (Incidentally, this clarifies the sense of verse 15 so as to render unnecessary a reordering of the parts of the verse.) It is not as though Edom fades from view at verses 15 and 16; it receives direct and explicit attention in verses 18, 19 and 21. This means that Edom can be regarded as included in 'all the nations' rather than separated off from them (a separation which has no theological point).

3. It is not at all implausible that there are two sorts of drinking referred to in the first two lines of the verse. 'As you Edomites drank in mad revelry on the mountain of *my* [outraged emphasis] holiness, so all the nations will drink of my wrath to the bitter end—and any thoughts of escape you have will prove to be utterly unfounded.' In fact, more can be said here. The very fact that, in contrast to almost every other biblical use of the image of drinking God's wrath (the one exception is Ps. 60:3), there is no mention of 'wrath' or of a particular vessel ('bowl' or 'cup') might suggest that it is not a single (sort of) drink which is referred to in the verse. In fact, taking this further, it is possible that the idea of the 'cup of the wine of wrath' might not even be present in the second half of the verse. The idea (in the absence of reference to 'cup' or 'wrath') might be that, just as the Edomites drank in mad and wicked revelry, so God will make all the nations (Edom included) drink and keep drinking, get drunk and more drunk until they are so utterly soaked that they pass from consciousness and never get up again. Although this would represent a judgement from God, it is a slightly different image from that of the 'cup of wrath'.

4. The place where the drinking took place gives no firm indication one way or another as to who did the drinking. The Edomites drank in revelry on the mountain of God's holiness and the people of Judah drank of God's wrath on the mountain of his holiness.

5. Attention has not been given to the fact that, if the 'you' of verse 16*a* were the people of Judah and the drinking were the drinking of God's wrath, this would be the only direct reference in the whole vision to the

guilt of God's people. Doubtless, the disaster which had befallen them was utterly deserved, but this is simply not the focus of Obadiah's prophecy. This strikes me as a strong argument for the 'you' referring to the Edomites and not to the people of Judah.

6. On another level, and perhaps unfairly, it could also be mentioned that, although modern commentators have sometimes sneered at those of an earlier age for their smoothing out apparent contradictions between biblical passages and for their explaining one passage by reference to another, they are not averse to their own sort of harmonization—that which flows from what has been called 'parallelomania'. It is clever and interesting to explore the 'cup of wrath' theme at the moment when Obadiah mentions 'drinking', but that does not mean that Obadiah is referring to it (at least, not necessarily in both parts of the verse).

I think that arguments B3 and B5 are my inventions, which means that I probably think they are better than they are. Nevertheless, my conclusion—arising from the inconclusiveness of the arguments to the contrary and from the neglect of argument B5 above—is that the Edomites are the 'you' of Obadiah 16a.

Acts 2, Joel 2 and Obadiah 17

Some have objected to the idea that Peter's use of Joel in Acts 2 helps us understand the part of Obadiah which Joel quotes because Peter stops his quotation from Joel (or Luke stops his account of Peter's quotation from Joel) precisely at the moment in Joel *before* Joel quotes Obadiah—'For in Mount Zion and in Jerusalem there shall be those who escape' (Joel 2:32). So, the objection runs, Peter's sermon doesn't help us understand Obadiah; in fact, it makes the interpretation of Obadiah *more* difficult.

Well, happily, in the sound archives we have come across a radio interview with Obadiah which took place in the early days after Pentecost. Here is a transcript ...

Interviewer. Following the news that there appear to be rifts in the new sect called Christians about how what has been going on relates to prophecies in the Hebrew Scriptures, we are going over to the prophet Obadiah who is in our radio car—in heaven. Obadiah, can you hear me? There seems to be an awful lot of noise in the background. What's going on?

Obadiah. Yes, John, I can just about hear you, but you'll have to speak up—there's a massive party taking place behind me. You heard what Jesus said about how much rejoicing there was in heaven over one sinner who repents—well, imagine it now with 3,000 converts from Pentecost! I've never seen or heard anything like it! The angel Gabriel is leading a conga round the gates; Enoch and Elijah are skating on the sea of glass and the rest of us, the disembodied spirits of the righteous, well, I'm not allowed to tell what we get up to. But it's more fun than you've ever had on a Tuesday morning, John.

Interviewer. Maybe so, but it can't have escaped your notice, Obadiah, that when Peter quoted Joel in his now-famous sermon on the day of Pentecost, he completely missed out the line where Joel in turn quoted you. That can't have been an accident, and many are saying that it was a deliberate snub from the new Gentile-philes to you Gentile-sceptics. How does it feel to be publicly put down like that?

Obadiah. Sorry, John, I can hardly hear you. How do I feel, did you ask? Well, it's obvious how I feel. This is absolutely wonderful—the new world has begun, the kingdom of God has been established, thousands of people are being reconciled to God—it is truly fantastic! I'm delighted—and so is every other prophet up here. Amazing stuff!

Interviewer. But I must press you on the point of Peter's deliberate snub. He blatantly omitted your words from his quotation of Joel. That can only be taken as a provocation, surely?

Obadiah. John, John, you journalists are all the same, aren't you? You're determined to find splits where none exist. Let me make two points absolutely clear. First, *of course* Peter left my words out of his quotation of Joel. Don't you remember who was there? People from every nation under heaven. If Peter had carried on to my words, then some of them would have been in danger of missing the point—they'd have thought that this was some revival of Jerusalem-obsessed parochialism. Now that's not what I said and not what I meant, and they'd have been badly mistaken to have thought that, and Peter knew that full well; but what's the point of saying things that might be misheard? He knew what he was doing—and I was listening to the whole address and I have to say that I loved every word of it. It's the same with the rest of the boys up here. Isaiah—he talked about the nations streaming up to Mount Zion to learn God's law. Ezekiel—he talked about the resurrection of the whole house of Israel. Zechariah talked about ten men from every language of the nations grasping the sleeve of a Jewish man. But does that mean that Isaiah or Ezekiel or Zechariah was put out by what Peter said? Not a bit of it. We are totally thrilled, utterly delighted, and we're having a complete riot up here!

Interviewer. But, surely—

Obadiah. No, John, please be patient. That's my first point. Second, can I say this for the benefit of all your listeners? It's important that this should be understood. Since what I said was quoted by Joel in a particular section of his prophecy and since Peter said that that section of his prophecy has been fulfilled, then even if Peter didn't quote my words, it's obvious, isn't it, that my words will be part of the same fulfilment moment too? It's not rocket science, John.

(Massive explosions and cheers in the background.)

Interviewer. More noise there—what's happening now?

Obadiah. You wouldn't believe it—journalists never do—but we just heard that another 2,000 people have been converted! Phenomenal! Oh my, Raphael and Uriel are throwing red giants around, and Michael's just picking up a couple of galaxies. It's fireworks time! I'm going to have to go.

Interviewer. Thank you, Obadiah. That was Obadiah the prophet.

Further resources

Accessible

Baker, David W., in **Baker, David W., Alexander, T. Desmond,** and **Waltke, Bruce K.,** *Obadiah, Jonah and Micah* (TOTC; Leicester: IVP, 1998)

Calvin, John, *Commentaries upon the Twelve Minor Prophets,* vol. ii: *Joel, Amos, Obadiah,* trans. John Owen (Edinburgh: Calvin Translation Society, 1846)

Craigie, Peter, *The Twelve Prophets,* vol. i (Daily Study Bible; Edinburgh: The St Andrew Press, 1984)

Henry, Matthew, *A Commentary upon the Whole Bible,* vol. iv (1712; [n.d.], Iowa Falls, IA: World Bible Publishers)

Hutcheson, George, *An Exposition of the Prophecies of Obadiah, Jonah, Micah, Nahum, Habakkuk and Zephaniah* (London, 1654)

Mid-level

Busenitz, Irvin A., *Joel and Obadiah* (Mentor Commentary; Fearn: Christian Focus, 2003)

The Geneva Bible, 1599

Keil, C. F., *Obadiah* (Keil-Delitzsch Commentary on the OT; Grand Rapids, MI: Eerdmans, 1988)

Marbury, Edward, *A Brief Commentarie or Exposition upon the Prophecy of Obadiah* (London, 1649)

Pusey, E. B., *The Minor Prophets* (1885; 1996, Barnes' Notes; Grand Rapids, MI: Baker)

Rainolds, John, *The Prophecie of Obadiah Opened and Applied* (Oxford, 1613)

Smith, G. A., *The Book of the Twelve Prophets,* vol. ii, 10th edn. (The Expositor's Bible; London: Hodder and Stoughton, 1908)

Trapp, John, *A Commentary or Exposition upon the XII Minor Prophets* (London, 1654)

Demanding

Allen, Leslie, *Joel, Obadiah, Jonah and Micah* (NICOT; Grand Rapids, MI: Eerdmans, 1976)

Barton, John, *Joel and Obadiah* (OTL; Louisville, KY: Westminster John Knox Press, 2001)

Ben Zvi, Ehud, 'A Historical-Critical Study of the Book of Obadiah', in *Beihefte zur ZAW,* 242(1996)

Bewer, J. A., *Obadiah and Joel* (ICC; Edinburgh: T&T Clark, 1911)

Clark, David J., and **Mundhenk, Norm,** *A Handbook on the Books of Obadiah and Micah* (UBS Helps for Translators; London: UBS, 1982)

Coggins, Richard J., *Israel Among the Nations: A Commentary on the Books of Nahum and Obadiah* (International Theological Commentary; Grand Rapids, MI: Eerdmans, 1985)

Further resources

Finley, Thomas J., *Joel, Amos, Obadiah: An Exegetical Commentary* ([n.p.]: Biblical Studies Press, 2003)

Mason, R., *Micah, Nahum, Obadiah* (Old Testament Guides; Sheffield: JSOT Press, 1991)

Niehaus, Jeffrey, *Obadiah*, in **McComiskey, Thomas E.** (ed.), *The Minor Prophets*, vol. ii (Grand Rapids, MI: Baker, 1993)

Raabe, Paul, *Obadiah* (Anchor Bible, 24D; New York: Doubleday, 1997)

Renkema, Johan, *Obadiah* (Historical Commentary on the Old Testament; Leuven: Peeters, 2003)

Stuart, Douglas, *Hosea–Jonah* (WBC; Waco, TX: Word, 1987)

Wade, G. W., *Micah, Obadiah, Joel and Jonah* (Westminster Commentaries; London: Methuen and Co., 1925)

Wolff, Hans Walter, *Obadiah and Jonah: A Commentary* (Minneapolis: Augsburg Publishing House, 1986)

Additionally, I have put online some more technical notes and extracts which can be found at http://www.davidpfield.com/obadiah.htm.